PERSPECTIVES, INSIGHTS & PRIORITIES

17 Leaders Speak Freely of Librarianship

Edited by
NORMAN HORROCKS

With a Foreword by
ED KURDYLA

The Scarecrow Press, Inc.
Lanham, Maryland • Toronto • Oxford
2005

SCARECROW PRESS, INC.

Published in the United States of America
by Scarecrow Press, Inc.
A wholly owned subsidiary of
The Rowman & Littlefield Publishing Group, Inc.
4501 Forbes Boulevard, Suite 200, Lanham, Maryland 20706
www.scarecrowpress.com

PO Box 317
Oxford
OX2 9RU, UK

British Library Cataloguing in Publication Information Available

Library of Congress Control Number: 2005925760

ISBN 0-8108-5355-8 (pbk. : alk. paper)

∞ ™ The paper used in this publication meets the minimum requirements of American National
Standard for Information Sciences—Permanence of Paper for Printed Library Materials, ANSI/
NISO Z39.48-1992. Manufactured in the United States of America.

CONTENTS

FOREWORD

ED KURDYLA

T HE IDEA FOR THIS BOOK arose during a breakfast meeting I had with Norman Horrocks. Indeed, it is safe to say that Norman was the inspiration. Despite being interrupted constantly by passersby, all of whom knew Norman and felt obliged to greet him, our discussion of issues large and small was wide ranging and lively, serious and humorous. While listening to Norman I realized that his wisdom and insight were treasures that must be preserved and passed on. While Norman in many ways is *sui generis*, I realized there were many other luminaries in the profession whose thoughts were important to all of us and to those who will follow. Not thoughts and ideas stemming from research or couched in scholarly essays, but personal thoughts, personal insights, evaluating their life's work—indeed, their lives—in terms of librarianship or the reverse.

Norman liked the idea. We appointed him editor and gave him a free hand to select a diverse group of contributors. Norman, in turn, gave the contributors a free hand to write whatever they wished, in any style or format they preferred. Honestly, we weren't quite sure what would result, how the essays would fit together, if they would fit together. Some contributors asked for a bit more guidance or structure, but we declined, arguing that placing the onus on them would result in a more personal, more forceful, and more honest contribution. We were right.

This extraordinary book defines and describes librarianship and library science through insightful essays contributed by seventeen recognized leaders of the profession. While each essay presents a unique perspective and approach, collectively they paint a picture of a humane and human profession central to and concerned with the cultural, social, political, and intellectual underpinnings of civilization. Often challenging and provocative, often moving, always engaging, the essays reflect a diverse and complex profession and the values, beliefs, practices, and philosophies that make it unique and vital.

The essays take a variety of approaches: historical analysis, personal recollection, career review, political or social commentary, intellectual or philosophical musings, short- and long-range forecasting. Even when the essays address issues of a practical nature, they raise issues of concern in a broader context. The role of libraries in a democratic society is examined through the historical perspective of the Boston Mandate of 1852, the most recent U.S. presidential election, and the current strain of censorship and battles over intellectual freedom. What is the proper role of libraries as social organizations advocating societal reform and working toward the common weal? What is the role of government and politics in the profession? What is the responsibility and role of the library in determining or advocating public policy? If, as one essay argues, our professional concern should center not on information or fact, but on truth, can we avoid political action and political repercussion? These are weighty issues addressed not only with passion, but with a freedom and honesty seldom encountered.

As this book was being prepared, I came across notes I took while attending my first ALA Annual Conference, in Detroit in 1977. I was a student at the University of Michigan School of Library Science, now the Library and Information Services Specialization (Library and Information Science) in the School of Information. I remember feeling challenged and frustrated, even angry, by what obviously was a failure of the citizenry to understand and appreciate the noble endeavors I planned to undertake in the coming years. I thought the questions and issues were simple and could be addressed and resolved simply. As I read and reconstructed the notes nearly three decades later, I was struck by my now ambivalent feelings toward many of the issues raised.

[From my notes:]

In a world where information is a driving force for economic, political, social, and cultural development librarianship should be recognized as one of the noblest, most significant, and most attractive professions. Librarians should be lionized, and they should be compensated accordingly. Instead, the general public misunderstands librarianship, at best, and the specific constituencies and communities they serve under value librarians too often. Among the major professions, and I believe librarianship is one of the few true professions in the traditional sense as defined a generation ago by the venerable International Encyclopedia of the Social Sciences, librarianship is, perhaps, the least materially rewarding. Among the true professions, librarianship arguably earns the least respect and status for its members.

Why is this true? Some have argued it is a failure of the leading professional associations, the American Library Association (ALA) in the United States being the most prominent and most culpable, to advocate for the significance of librarianship in society. Others have argued that library science, itself, lacks the intellectual foundation and rigor necessary to qualify as a science and the philosophical structures necessary to qualify as a bona fide academic discipline and the basis of a profession.

Needless to say, the issues remain, as do many others related to and intertwined with them. The Issues & Advocacy section of the ALA website delineates several topics:

Accreditation; Advocacy for Libraries; CIPAexpand; Diversity; Education and Continuing Learning; Ethics; Human Resources; Intellectual Freedom/Censorship; International Relations; Literacy; Outreach; Recruitment; Best Practices

While most of the issues and topics above are addressed in the essays in this book, there are no simple answers and conclusions presented. I believe, however, that most readers will draw conclusions and recognize many de facto values, beliefs, ideas, and ideals that have evolved to define librarianship.

This is a powerful and important book. Every librarian, every library student, every public official should read it, as indeed should every citizen concerned with his or her community.

From Oral Tradition to Electronic: Accessing and Disseminating Information

ISMAIL ABDULLAHI

THE FIRST AND EARLIEST PERIOD of human communication was one in which orality, or the "oral tradition," was dominant. The second period emerged with the development of print, or written communication. The third major development came with electronic media, the "information age."

In orality, speaking and listening are the central activities. Print requires writers and readers. Electronic media requires organized production and viewers. In other words, in each historical era of communication, control of communication mechanisms has varied significantly. These controls moved from the individual face-to-face encounter of oral to the distant, depersonalized, and passive role of communication recipients in the electronic era. This essay will discuss the evolution of my experience with these three areas of communication and provide a greater understanding of the role played by these types of communications in our societies.

Oral communication is slow, moving from one person to another in a deliberate and time-consuming manner. Before the advent of communication technologies such as writing instruments and printing, oral tradition remained the primary means of passing knowledge from one generation to the next. It still remains as a way of communication in many parts of Africa, Asia, and Latin America. Oral tradition represents the transmission of knowledge from one individual to another and one generation to another through speaking, listening, and memorization. In oral societies, culture and customs were transferred from one individual to the next and one generation to the next in the form of stories, myths, rituals and ceremonies. It is a way of transferring people's cultural history and ancestry. They serve the place of modern educational institutions and libraries. I remember when I was a child, my grandfather Awe Ali "Grandpa Ali" who was a noted oral historian tried unsuccessfully to disseminate some of our ancestral heritage to us

I

his grandchildren. Like my older brothers, I was quite convinced that the way to future success lay through published information sources accessed through educational institutions. In our many conversations, my grandfather was truly embarrassed by how little we knew about our ancestral culture and history. The generation change from oral pedagogy to the written word occurred during my generation in Africa as new urban communities whose kids attended modern educational institutions learned how to read rather than listen, to show allegiance to print communication rather than spoken words. As far as my family and ancestors are concerned it was a time of transition from oral information that included our distinctive heritage to alien published information mainly about European history and culture. This created the social, political, and historical discontinuity among the first generation that received formal education and that of the traditionally trained generation of my father. This trend continues in urban African societies.

An important aspect of all three areas of communication is the transmission or dissemination of knowledge. Similar to that of African societies is that of Native American groups who heavily relied on oral tradition to transmit knowledge from one generation to the next pertaining to a variety of issues. One such group is the Cherokee tribe. The Cherokee tradition involves the character of a "Trickster," often a figure from nature such as a rabbit. Within the Cherokee oral tradition, the story of the rabbit races with turtle is one in which the Trickster rabbit is defeated not by the plodding nature of the turtle but by means of guile. In this story the rabbit challenges turtle to a race in which the winner will be declared the more intelligent of the two. Rabbit is convinced his speed will ensure victory over the plodding, deliberate Turtle. Turtle, however, realizes his speed cannot match the Rabbit's but his intellect and ability to out-think Rabbit will win the race. The implicit message of the story is that there are times when it is important to use the mind rather than the body to achieve a desired outcome. The trickster stories were an important part of Cherokee tradition, because it illustrates the tribal belief that there are forces of mischief in the world. Man, according to Cherokee beliefs, lives in harmony with nature, but he is often called into conflict with nature and with forces beyond his immediate understanding. Oral tradition helped individuals deal with unexplained forces in life and provide hope for the future.

Chanting, singing, oration, storytelling and other forms of oral tradition helped pass knowledge from one generation to the next. These forms of oral transmission included practical information such as survival skills, medicine, cooking, making of clothes, hunting and other information. Elders were often vital for such dissemination of information since they were older and embodied most knowledge. In traditional societies such as in Africa, they did have information specialists. Information was readily available as a result of the pedagogical and information function of elders and other knowledgeable individuals. Individuals like my grandfather Awe Ali and those of West Africa known as the *Griots* were noted knowledge holders in their societies and functioned as indigenous libraries. They also function as libraries because they can easily move to places where dissemination of information is needed. Through the stories they provide, they interconnect the values of the past and the present. However, the oral tradition must be practiced in order to endure. Passing information by word of mouth runs the risk of different interpretations, forgetting, and even extinction from lack of practice. Because of this risk, the people I belong to "the Oromo people" divide their society into age-grades apprenticeship called the "Gada System." Gada is an eight-year cyclical system that gives equal opportunity to everyone to learn about their tradition until the age of forty. Learning from the elders and transferring information to the new generation is part of the culture and tradition.

The evolution of written communication required a number of inventions from writing instruments and paper as we know it to printing presses that enable mass publication. Ancient civilizations like the Phoenicians and Sumerians developed an alphabet and cuneiform writing respectively. Cuneiform represented pictorial depictions of information. The Egyptians developed a form of writing known as hieroglyphics, a more elaborate and developed form of communication than the Phoenicians or Sumerians.

The advent of written communication replaced oral communications as a main form of recorded history and information dissemination, primarily because of its greater permanence. The advent of written communication also necessitated the ability to read whatever language or form of written communication was recorded. In 1436 the invention of the printing press by Johannes Gutenberg transformed written communication, making printed written communication more accessible to the masses. This was because the invention of the printing press not only reduced the price of printed materials but it also permitted mass production of printed resources. For nearly 500 years, Gutenberg's printing press and its successors shaped the form and nature of written communication. It took little more than three decades for printing to spread across Europe. Printing greatly enhanced the ability of written communication to enlighten and transform culture and dissemination of information, especially that of the western hemisphere. It became the catalyst for the renaissance, the humanist rebirth, the cultural, political revolution, and the mass production of literature and the opening of libraries and the transformation of societies as far away as Africa, Asia, and Latin America.

The advent of electronic media—the telegraph, radio, TV, and finally the Internet brought new opportunities for ordinary people to gain greater and greater access to information and knowledge. At the same time it can be argued that modern mass electronic media render the recipient of such material more passive and less active than either oral or written communications. In oral communications, the interaction between one communicator and the other was immediate and direct. In early print communication, both sender and receiver required certain skills and a certain level of desire to participate in the exchange of or receipt of information. Today, with electronic media proliferating at a rapid rate, and with the exception of the Internet, communication is more one-way than two-way. This is, of course, a trend that began to be observed in the era of print and which technology has furthered dramatically.

During the nineteenth and twentieth centuries, inventions like the telegraph, telephone, motion pictures, cameras, TV, and the Internet radically transformed the ability to disseminate information to mass audiences. Access to such information was also greatly enhanced by these forms of electronic communication. The need for access to information from anywhere in the world helped spur the development of computers, the Internet, and modern digital technologies. The Internet provides access to information and can disseminate information more rapidly, less expensively, and to more people than ever before in human history. It has revolutionized communication as much from its diverse capabilities as its innovation. The Internet has rapidly transformed the ways in which people communicate as well as providing access to information of enormous content and diversity. Whole libraries and librarians are now available online to be consulted.

Internet technology has also enabled grassroots political campaigns to gain momentum like never before. Multimedia applications enable communication that is highly sophisticated, involving pictures, video streams, music, color, text, and other components of communication. The Internet also reduces many barriers associated with written or printed communication, including geographic location, time constraints, costs and others. Such inventions continue to transform the way people communicate the world over.

Despite the radically different nature of oral tradition from electronic communication, historians relate electronic communication's roots to that of the ancient forms of communication of the days when homing pigeons carried messages for the Greeks. Today, wireless technologies offer a much more reliable form of message carrying but have evolved from the desire of individuals and societies to communicate. This communication involves not only information dissemination in the here-and-now but also information about previous generations and cultures. Digital technologies, including wireless transmission of information, continue to be developed that will provide greater ability to disseminate and retrieve information among peoples. This review of communication from oral tradition to electronic technologies demonstrates that throughout human history cultures have tried to share information by the most advanced means possible. It is likely that new forms of communication will continue to evolve because of the human desire for information sharing, though the change is not for everyone on the planet because not every society has equal opportunity to access information or possess the tools required for access. The more information technologies are created the more information gaps they bring. Only a few can access these technologies, which means others are left without them, thus creating the vicious circle of underdevelopment and poverty.

Libraries have been involved in providing access to information for people for a very long time. They were able to integrate and deal with massive technological and societal changes that have taken place in the past. Among many challenges that libraries of the future face are those of dealing with the "served" and the "underserved" population. Some of them might represent the "technologically displaced" people such as: the economically displaced, the elderly, the unemployed, or the less educated. When dealing with these problems library school curricula should include a component related to humanistic concerns that provide a foundation of library education of the future. More importantly, library schools must increase their efforts to recruit more students of color from diverse populations to increase diversity among professionals to fulfill the information needs mentioned above.

Information professionals of the future should also continue to promote effective human relations through providing information to individuals, groups, organizations, and different people. Future librarians must have the skills to work with different people of diverse background and be sensitive to their needs. They should be able to create a better understanding between people, cultures, civilizations that will contribute to the peaceful co-existence among the people of the world.

Suggested Readings

Bellis, M (2004). "A Brief History of Writing Instruments." Viewed June 1, 2004, http://inventors.about.com/library/weekly/aa100197.htm, 1–3.

——— (2004). "Johannes Gutenberg and the Printing Press." Viewed June 1, 2004, http://inventors.about.com/library/inventors/blJohannesGutenberg, 1–2

Champlin, D., and J. Knoedler (June 2002). "Operating in the Public Interest or in Pursuit of Private Profits." *Journal of Economic Issues* 36(2), 459–469.

Dillon, K. (2002). "Preserving the Past through Oral Tradition." Viewed June 1, 2004, http://akak.essortment.com/oraltradition/rjrr.htm, 1–2.

"History of the Information Revolution and Communications Technology Timeline." Viewed June 1, 2004, http://myron.sjsu.edu/caesars/com.htm, 1–8.

The Library Professional

CAMILA ALIRE

"What is more important in a library than anything else—than everything else—is the fact that it exists."

—ARCHIBALD MACLEISH, 1892–1982

OUR LIBRARIES' EXISTENCE should not be taken for granted. Libraries, no matter the type, are critical to our democratic society. How we provide library services is critical because people will vote with their feet. How we engage our community and encourage use of our libraries is important because, today, people have many more choices, which compete with the library.

In writing about my philosophy/personal view of librarianship, it was a challenge to narrow my thoughts. What have I learned in the practice of librarianship in the past that should help in the future? To answer that question, I had to categorize my thoughts into two areas: the profession and the professional.

The Profession

Libraries provide an information service. What we do, how we do it, and who benefits are all questions tied to library information services.

If I have learned anything from the past I have overheard that the overall *what* we do rarely changes. We have, for centuries, provided access to information through some type of library. Libraries are about providing information for our patrons to make them a more informed populace, and that will not change.

What is inevitable is changing *how* we provide information. Our modern society demands that libraries keep up with the times. Although the book is still revered by many, our Generation Xers and our Millennials (Generation Y) are expecting much more from libraries in order for them to become library users or to be sustained as library users. Their information is "googled"; the process of finding that information is googling; and if it is googled, it must be true.

So the *how* of providing library services requires libraries and their staffs to be responsive and flexible. Our profession and our libraries are changing. Libraries don't change themselves, people change them. And what I have learned is that change is not easy in our profession. If I have any advice for library administrators, it would be that understanding and preparing for the role of a change agent should not be underestimated. Preparing library staff and library users for change needs to be systematic and timely. A quote by King Whitney Jr., president, at the time, of Personnel Laboratory Inc., is most appropriate:

> Change has considerable psychological impact on the human mind. To the fearful, it is threatening because it means that things may get worse. To the hopeful, it is encouraging because things may get better. To the confident, it is inspiring because the challenge exists to make things better. Obviously, then, one's character and frame of mind determine how readily he brings about change and how he reacts to change that is imposed on him.[1]

Many situations dictate the need for transformation. Reflecting on the past, I maintain that technology and funding challenges continue to dictate how we do business in our libraries. That is not going to change in the near future. We like the convenience that library technology provides us. Many of us, however, would still prefer holding the print version in our hands. We also like the convenience of accessing information 24/7 in our pajamas in the privacy of our homes. And, again, many of us would prefer to print out that information to read it.

Because the library profession today seems synonymous with transformation, my advice as a seasoned practitioner to library leaders is that they need to accept their roles as change agents; they need to be hopeful and confident. My advice to librarians and other library staff is that they have to recognize the need to stay in pace with changing times and environments; their characters or frames of mind will shape their reactions to changing libraries.

So who will benefit from our library services? In order to answer that from my perspective, I have to acknowledge that I have learned and observed much from the past. I have found that libraries serve predominantly the middle- and upper-class communities. These communities have been important to libraries in the past.

So much of the time, when we equate libraries with a democratic society, we tend to concentrate on issues dealing with the First Amendment—freedom of speech and ideas. Accessing information is almost as important as the information itself. For me, equal access means that information in a public library is available to everyone. More specifically, what that means is that libraries should provide equal opportunity for everyone to use that information. However, equity of access deals with the fairness of encouraging that access. One of the most significant transformations of libraries from centuries ago has been the shift from being an institution for the privileged to being free and open to all people. This has been most apparent as the literacy rate has increased dramatically throughout the centuries. Once only aristocrats, academics, and clergy were literate and, thus, the collectors of books. There was no need for public libraries. As books became more readily available, the general populace became more literate, which in turn led to the establishment of libraries. Today, in our democratic society, libraries should be more proactive not only in providing access, but also in reaching out and encouraging access to all segments of our literate society.

Along with the growing population in the United States comes a population of underserved communities. Our changing demographics reflect a significant growth in minority residents, but our libraries are not reflecting an adjustment to that demographic change. And, if some are, it is not enough.

How would my perspective affect the future of our profession and of libraries? What we have now is a growing society of disenfranchised minority residents who do not understand that libraries are essential to our democratic society. Along with our Generation X and Y public, these are our future leaders, who will be making decisions about library funding either as voters, trustees, city councils, or boards of regents.

I am an eternal optimist. I believe library professionals will rise to the occasion and not only recognize the importance of outreach to our country's underserved minority community, but will do something about it. I am expecting our Generation Xers and Millennials to have an increased social consciousness, which includes the importance of meeting the information needs of this minority segment of our society. What they will find is that minorities have the same information needs as the rest of our society, needs that could help develop sound coping, job, and consumer education skills. We, minorities, have high hope for ourselves. We hope and want to better our personal and familial situations. We hope and want our children to be well educated. Libraries need to reach out and demonstrate to us that part of being well-educated means that our children should also be information literate. As a library professional, I know the importance of information literacy, but many minority families do not.

In reflecting on our wonderful library profession, what I have learned from the past that can be applied to the future is that, as we continue to provide library services, we will need to change how we do it to fit the changing needs of our society. We will need to reach out to other segments of our society—our underserved minority communities—so that they may benefit from our information services. And until we do that, we will continue to have a disenfranchised populace in this democratic society.

The Library Professional

For me, professionalism is a state of mind. So when I refer to the "library professional," I mean anyone who works in a library. I don't mean to diminish the importance of the MLS degree, but as a library administrator, my expectations are for all library staff to act professionally. In this essay, I am going to focus mostly on the librarian.

I have a lot to share with librarians, which will hopefully help them in the future. There are two areas of advice I want to share. The first is how to deal successfully with change. The other is what I call the "Triple I traits": innovation, impact, and integrity—all essential elements of success in our great profession.

Earlier in this essay, I referred to our ever-changing profession. Librarians who embrace change are hopeful because they see the possibility for things to improve whether they are the change agents or part of the transformation process. Challenging times for our libraries inspire librarians and library leaders to make situations better.

I am not a proponent of change for change's sake. The library professional must understand that our profession is dynamic and that circumstances, usually beyond our control, may require changing the way we do things in our libraries. For so long, our profession has been static and, consequently, has provided a safe and comfortable zone for many librarians. This sense of comfort has drawn many people to our profession and/or has kept them working in libraries. Consequently, when circumstances require our libraries to change, there is usually some internal disorder.

My experiences have taught me two things about the transformation of our libraries: (1) change is difficult to implement in a library when the people in that organization are most comfortable with the status quo, and (2) it takes confident people who are not afraid to take risks to implement change. To transform a library, the first step is to prepare the library staff for change even before it begins. Staff involvement from the beginning is important, and constant communication is critical before, during, and after the transformation.

Change is inevitable given the technological and funding challenges libraries face. How can library professionals be prepared to deal not only with change, but also with the everyday operations of our libraries in the future? Based on experiences of the past, I maintain that the library profession would be best served by librarians and other library workers who understand and practice the Triple I traits. Innovation, impact, and integrity, when embodied in librarians' everyday practices, no matter their positions within the libraries, can help shape our libraries of tomorrow.

Innovation is essential and must be sustained. If I am correct in saying that change will continue to be a part of our professional lives, then how we handle that change is important. In libraries, innovation not only includes assessing the current practice in the context of a changing environment, but also doing something about it. Librarians need to think outside the box and push the envelope until a new or revised practice and/or service surfaces. We need to demonstrate a "what if" mentality, asking the question when complacency starts affecting our services or when a challenge arises. In the train of library services, complacency is the caboose, and innovation is the engine pushing forward to meet the information needs of all of our society—rich and poor, urban and rural, majority and minority.

Impact is the second Triple I trait. It has been my experience that, no matter the status of librarians or other library workers, impact of their work and their actions can be significant. By impact I mean *making a difference*. We are in the business of providing information services. Each one of us working in libraries has the opportunity to make a difference in someone's life whether that person is in our community, schools, or universities. As an academic library administrator, I can make a difference by leading my academic library into improving our services to our students, faculty, and staff. The person working in interlibrary loan can make a difference by assisting doctoral students in their research/review of the literature. The instruction librarian can make a difference by making sure that every university graduate leaves with information literacy skills. The impact of what we do and how we could do it better should not be underestimated.

Integrity is the third quality in my Triple I traits. From the past, I have learned that integrity should drive what we do as library professionals. I have a copy of a saying taped to a file cabinet in my office that I have carried from job to job. It reads "Once you lose your integrity, everything else is a piece of cake." For me, integrity is multidimensional. I am writing about personal integrity, professional integrity, and integrity of the process.

Personal and professional integrity go hand in hand. You can't separate them. Your personal integrity is what shapes your professional integrity. We find ourselves in challenging times in our libraries; we are competing with other services for the same shrinking dollar, where more is expected of us, where what we do is challenged in the courts, or where we might be asked to compromise ourselves. We have to make hard decisions, and those decisions should be driven by our professional integrity.

Those hard decisions should also be driven by the integrity of the process. Were you fair, and were you consistent in the process of making the decision? If you can sleep at night after the decision is made because the integrity of the process prevailed, then you have nothing to worry about.

Conclusion

Although libraries are key to our democratic society, they are still a privilege, unfortunately, and not a fundamental right. I would not disagree with Archibald MacLeish that the most important thing about libraries is that they exist. However, library professionals, cannot be complacent about taking our libraries for granted. The beauty about the past is that what we learn from it can help us shape our future. And that past is only successful if it ignites action to improve the future. Our challenge from the past is to make sure that *all segments* of our society, now and in the future, become information literate by understanding, appreciating, and using our libraries.

Library professionals have exciting times ahead of them. Libraries will continue to transform to meet the information needs of our society. Library professionals will not only realize the importance of reaching out to serve our underserved communities, but will also be proactive in doing so. Innovation, impact, and integrity will be integrated qualities utilized by library professionals to assist them through their everyday working lives.

Note

1. *Wall Street Journal*, June 1967.

Election 2004: The Library Fails Again

JOHN N. BERRY III

T
HE DEPRESSING U.S. ELECTION of 2004 was over. It wasn't just the results that sent me into the slough of despond. The endless campaign had done fatal damage to my trust in government and politicians, and had shown how politics can trump principle when it comes to standards of accuracy and context in information.

In New England, where I live, the election was the first icy blast of the winter wind that would spread a leafless grayness over our landscape. Truth lay bleeding in the aftermath. A regional despair lasted for several days. Most people felt disenfranchised, and injured by the election. Many felt dirtied, corrupted by the campaign.

I let my own standards of truth telling fall by default. As a librarian I thought of myself as a champion of the idea that information gives democracy the immunity that protects it from the often-terminal diseases of political corruption and ideological extremism. But I had not worked on the campaign. I had not used the platform that was still mine to comment on the growing abuse of information. I had not rigorously applied a standard of objectivity to the information I used in discussions of the election issues with people who held other views; trying to undermine their position or to convert them to mine took a higher priority than rigorous pursuit of full information.

My depression had been building for months, even years. After all, I had watched as several U.S. administrations had dismantled huge sections of our government information apparatus. The government had destroyed a great deal of the record and locked up the rest. It had given the key to its own ideological and political spin doctors and/or to the attorney general and the other officials in whose hands the authority to manage information would be used as a weapon against their enemies. I had done little, written less on these issues.

I had paid attention to the "mainstream" media, only to see how obviously they had been infected by their insatiable hunger for popularity and profit. Newspapers, television, and the lot had been totally corrupted and were owned by or otherwise beholden to the high priests of their religion, entrepreneurial capitalism, preaching a kind of extreme laissez faire view of society. I had said nothing, written no editorial nor letter to any medium to try to expose what I knew was the truth. Corporate advertisers and owners, political donors, and religious and ideological "leaders" had tainted the communications apparatus of the entire society. The electorate had been overwhelmed with a torrent of information abuse. What facts were not spun to feed the prejudices of one side or the other, were ripped out of their context, or simply invented, all to win votes and attack the character and record of candidates.

The campaign had totally polluted the mainstream of information, and the few little alternative rills and rivulets that remained out of that mainstream were so totally biased and narrow in their outlook that they could be dismissed as the work of crackpots and zealots of right or left, or too narrowly focused to encompass or comprehend the complexities of the larger view of society. There was no corrective cleansing of the information pollution, no filters to remove the lies and distortions, so the voters were left with only misinformation, spin, or lack of information brought about by government censorship, commercially driven suppression, and monopoly ownership of information sources.

I am a librarian, and my depression deepened at the realization that my own profession had failed the electorate too. Sure, libraries had broad collections, and librarians were strong supporters of intellectual freedom and free access to information. Indeed, to their credit the librarians, organized under the banner of the American Library Association (ALA), had fought the government over the excesses of the Patriot Act and its intrusion on the citizen privacy that protects information seeking from the guilt by association that had marked other periods of reaction in U.S. history.

On the other hand, I was certain that library service would have collapsed if 1,000 library users, taxpaying citizens in any community, had sought deep information on any of the issues they were expected to decide by voting in the election. I knew, too, that few, if any, libraries had advertised or publicized the fact that their digital services and print collections could provide citizens with all the information they needed to understand and decide the urgent questions on our nation's agenda.

I knew that few libraries, if any, had systematically set out to correct the misinformation that was everywhere during the campaign. Few libraries had tried to collect the opposing views on every issue, or responses to the campaign books that oozed out of the usual propaganda publishers, publishing houses that have always specialized in delivering one side of the story. Indeed, I had seen some evidence that librarians and libraries in many communities had avoided collecting digital, print, or multi-media materials with views that might have been considered controversial in their communities. In a few extreme cases, the delivery of controversial information had even been suppressed by librarians and local officials. For example, library showings of Michael Moore's film *Fahrenheit 9/11* were cancelled or postponed until after the election due to adverse reactions from local officials in several U.S. communities.

I was also haunted by the suspicion that the library, like other information sources, was being lured by private donations, "partnerships" they were often called, into a corrupt relationship with commercial interests. Most libraries were under pressure to raise private money, and I had watched that effort change the priorities and orientation of a few. Some had become playthings of wealthy donors, and others had adopted the marketing schemes of hucksters to lure users and donors as you would customers for a product.

Throughout all of this my thoughts kept returning to some of the founding documents of our library profession. The words from one of them resounded in my mind through all of September and October. The quotation I couldn't shake from my consciousness came from *Upon the Objects to Be Attained by the Establishment of a Public Library*, that magnificent "Report of the Trustees of the Public Library of the City of Boston. 1852." That document truly set out the mandate for the public library movement in the United States. Here is the passage from page 15 that haunted me throughout the U.S. election campaign:

> For it has been rightly judged that—under political, social, and religious institutions like ours—it is of paramount importance that the means of general information should be so diffused that the largest possible number of persons should be induced to read and understand questions going down to the very foundations of social order, which are constantly presenting themselves, and which we, as a people, are constantly required to decide, and do decide, either ignorantly or wisely.

The Boston trustees went on to say that there was no doubt "that this can be done" and, as we know now, they proceeded to do it. Alas, it was on the steps of that great Boston Public Library that John Kerry had planned to celebrate his victory.

Libraries didn't have much impact on the presidential election or the campaign that preceded it. The diffusion of full information on those questions the electorate is required to decide was not apparent. Indeed, that mandated diffusion of information on current issues from libraries has never materialized. The incomplete information that was forthcoming to the voters, for the most part, did not come from libraries. The few libraries that had deep collections on the political issues facing the United States waited passively for inquiries from voters. There was little or no library effort at diffusion.

If the exalted idea that citizens should be "induced" to read up on the questions before our society was ever part of the library mission in the United States, it was abandoned long ago. Libraries have always been passive players in our political and social lives. Even the great library historian, Jesse Shera, who was among the first to celebrate that Boston document and make it an appendix to his *Foundations of the Public Library* (University of Chicago Press, 1949), asserted that the mandate and dream of Boston was never realized. On page 248 of that great work he said, "Judged by every standard and measured by every criterion, the public library is revealed as a social agency dependent upon the objectives of society. It followed—it did not create—social change." So public libraries have always followed society, according to Shera. The Boston mandate was only an ideal, abandoned before it was ever tried. Libraries didn't and still don't create change. They have never fully diffused the information citizens have needed to govern themselves, to fully understand the issues on the nation's agenda, even when the information to do that work has been there inside the library.

As for *inducing* citizens to read and understand those issues, only a very few of we timid librarians have ever dared to even attempt that challenge. We have not even dared to tell the citizens that they need to know the truth, and that we have it in our collections and services. There have been only occasional programs and intermittent local efforts to get people to inform themselves.

This is the civic failure of the public library in America, in the world. Librarians have been excellent servants, effective instructors in information seeking, great builders of diverse and deep collections, but they have not confronted the citizens with this reservoir of information. With a few rare and courageous exceptions, librarians have been afraid to go to the streets, to the meeting halls, to the "homes of the young" and the "cheap boarding houses" as the Boston trustees outlined the job.

This signal failure of librarianship has surely been one factor in the awful result that libraries have been relegated to the position of a sideshow in our public affairs, like the museums with which our current national government has paired them. It has meant that in community after community libraries have faced endless budget cuts, repeated neglect, and a position among the second rank of social institutions. Good public libraries are widely regarded as symbols of culture and education, museums of the mind, but rarely, if ever, as crucial tools of democratic self-government.

If we are to survive, this passive, symbolic role must change. It will not be easy to convince a profession so long accustomed to its uncontroversial, passive role as information helper and collector to become an active participant in public debate. It will not be easy to convince the citizens that they need this only uncorrupted information resource as the antidote to the poisons of bias, suppression, spin, and propaganda that could be so fatal to democracy. It will not be comfortable to provide information and viewpoints that may oppose the majority of citizens in a community. It will not be easy to convince them that truth and justice require that they allocate precious tax money to that purpose.

It will not be easy to make the public library a primary tool for citizen information and democratic decision making. It will not be easy, but it must be done to insure the survival of libraries and democracy.

Reflections on Librarianship: Values, Ethics and Practice

TONI CARBO

THE JOURNEY FROM a bibliographic assistant in a special library in 1962 to a professor and former dean at a university in 2004 has been a long and circuitous one that started with many questions and has resulted in a few answers, but even more questions. In reflecting on what has been of importance in the field, what comes to mind most are: people, values, and ethics. Of course, there have also been many forces, such as economic pressures, technological changes, management developments, that have helped to shape the nature of the discipline of library and information science (LIS) and the practice of the profession; however, I think these are less important. Over my long career, I have been enormously fortunate to have worked in, used, and visited hundreds of libraries around the world. Whether it was a tiny library in a refurbished firehouse in a small town in Colorado, a specialized science library, a school library, the Library of Congress, or one of many different libraries in numerous foreign countries, I have observed many of the same values and similar ethical issues. The basic elements of the practice are also often similar.

People

People have been the strength of librarianship as the field has continued to attract individuals with vision, who care about high quality service, meeting people's needs, preserving culture, and protecting societal values and civil liberties. I have had the honor and privilege of working with hundreds of outstanding individuals in libraries, archives, information industry companies, universities, and governments. These individuals come from diverse backgrounds, countries, and cultures, attracted by our profession because of the chance to make a difference in people's lives. It has been inspiring to talk with librarians who proudly show off their small community libraries, or fight for information policies at the highest level of government, or work to acquire and organize outstanding special collections, or develop cutting-edge new information systems, or run outstanding services for children or other special populations. What are most important in our field are the people who have made it the profession it is today. They share a vision of service and a set of values.

Values and Ethics

Values are fundamental to our profession; values are often what attracted individuals to the profession in the first place; and values form the basis of the education of our future colleagues. Rafael Capurro has reminded us that values are part of ". . . the background of various forms of living." Each of us develops a set of values over time from our family, friends, religious training, education, and society more widely. They are core beliefs that help us establish what we think is right or wrong. They are subjective and have their roots in rules, frequently as part of our religious and/or political beliefs (e.g., the Ten Commandments or the U.S. Declaration of Independence). Values often change over time as we are exposed to new ideas and different people and cultures, and as we experience and learn. Lencioni reminds us that there are many types of values, including corporate, core (deeply engrained principles), aspirational (those currently lacking, but needed for success), or even accidental (those that arise spontaneously, usually reflecting the common interests or personalities of employees). These form "la petite histoire"—our own personal story, the "baggage" we carry with us throughout life—often changing and usually evolving over time.

Getting agreement across our diverse profession about core values is very difficult, if not impossible, as the recent Report of ALA's Core Values Task Force II demonstrates. The work of the Task Force and many studies over time identify clusters, or "domains," of values, including: access, collaboration, diversity, education, intellectual freedom, preservation, privacy, professionalism, public good, and service. These are not values, themselves, of course, but they do indicate the areas, often overlapping, related to the core values. I find this list rather frustrating, because the topics are very vague and not really values; for example, "access" itself is not a value, but providing equal opportunity of access to information sources is a value. Other studies have identified additional values, some of which might well be included under the broad domains listed by the Task Force.

- Respecting intellectual property rights
- Treating colleagues with respect

- Safeguarding rights of employees
- Distinguishing between personal convictions and professional duties
- Maintaining professional neutrality
- Providing a balanced collection
- Maintaining the role of the librarian as teacher more than information provider

Fundamental Moral Experience

In examining codes of ethics from LIS organizations (defined very broadly to include such groups as the Society of Professional Journalists), as we do in my course on information ethics, we find significant similarities and some striking differences. Many codes begin with what we define as the Fundamental Moral Experience (FME), which is rooted not just in the head, but also in the heart, as Greek ethics has taught us. This experience involves three components: (1) affectivity—arising from feelings and emotions—a part of ethical reflection, which sometimes begins in awe and proceeds to reason; (2) hope—faith in someone, the desire for good for another person, a process that evolves; and (3) tolerance (from *tolere*, Latin for "to carry," as in to carry or support someone). Ethical reflection and language express the experience of each person's value of the individual. The experience is distinctly human and humanizing, and we all know of examples of exactly the opposite in such horrors as the Nazis determining that Jews were "subhuman," or in slavery, which effected the same dehumanization of people. It is the FME that provides the ability to see and respond to another person, and which is basic and essential to the values that we profess and try to live by.

Codes of Ethics as Guides

Building on the FME and on values, librarians strive to reflect ethically and take moral actions in their daily personal and professional lives. Codes of ethics or ethical guidelines are helpful roadmaps, but each of us struggles to learn the territory, determine where we want to go, and find the best way there. To determine "where we want to go," we need to start with our values. It is striking that the ALA Task Force identifies twenty questions, beginning with "What is a library?" The questions include: "How would you define ethical behavior for library and information professionals?" "What do you think these values are?" and "Do you have any personal values that conflict with your professional values?" Responding to the question "What is a library?" takes me to Ranganathan's Five Laws of Library Science from 1931 in which he reminds us that "the library is a growing organism." This law with the four others—books are for use, every book its reader, every reader his book, and save the reader's time—provides a very useful map for the territory of librarianship. Of course, one needs to expand "book" to all information sources, "his" to his or her, and "reader" to user and potential user in the "growing organism."

Education and Learning

With our values, which we must continue to examine and update, and Ranganathan's Five Laws as a map to help learn the territory, we can begin our journey. The next important pieces to guide us are our professional education and our experience. In identifying what has been of importance in the field during my professional career, the development of educational programs—both formal, graduate programs and continuing education programs—ranks very highly in significance. Having worked at four different universities and having taught, lectured, or served on external review panels at numerous others, I have participated in and observed the evolution of LIS programs for many years. The changes in our educational programs in more than forty years have been enormous. Some programs have died; others have started; all have changed, some dramatically. Each program strives to succeed by focusing on these critical factors: quality, centrality to the mission of the university, contribution of knowledge to the discipline, education of excellent professionals, and service to the profession and the wider community. Each program has taken on these challenges in different ways, many by embracing new technologies; others by building or adding undergraduate programs; some by adding other specialties; others by merging with other units into large colleges or schools; and many by developing distance education programs. Leadership of the programs has changed over the years with many more women being named dean or director and with many people from disciplines outside librarianship being brought in as well.

When I selected Drexel for my master's degree, I did so because I wanted to attend the best school and to learn the new technologies. It was in the required introductory course that I first learned about the field of bibliometrics, which led me to citation studies, scientific and technical communication, and, eventually, information policy. As it focused on its centrality to the mission of Drexel University, the college worked to be a leader in research related to information technology and in educating leaders for the information sciences and technology, including librarians. The M.S. degree provided a sound background for work in libraries and also for careers in the information industry. For me, after completing the first Ph.D. from Drexel's College, the degrees provided an excellent background for work in a nonprofit organization of indexing and abstracting services working to use the newest technologies to create electronic versions of their publications and make the databases available for searching, then at the Institution of Electrical Engineers in London with its publishing and database division, later at a U.S. government agency advising the president and Congress on policy and planning in the information field, and finally in a position as dean and professor in a large and diverse school with an LIS program. I chose to go to Pittsburgh because of its strong LIS program, its excellent information sciences (IS) program—combined in 1964 as the Graduate School of Library and Information Sciences—and the opportunity to build a new telecommunications program.

Undergraduate Programs

Drexel, Pittsburgh, and Syracuse were among the first schools to have undergraduate programs, not in librarianship, but in information science to educate people to work, often in corporations, on developing information systems or as software engineers. Many schools have since added undergraduate programs to meet the demands of the marketplace. Having undergraduate programs has expanded the schools into new areas and has opened opportunities for them to build collaborative programs with other units, such as schools of business or colleges of arts and sciences. These undergraduate programs have also increased the schools' visibility on campuses, provided new recruitment potential, and opened other doors, such as shared funding from athletics and participation in undergraduate student organizations and publications. Of course, this addition has also placed new demands on the schools for recruitment at the high school level and for greater collaboration with undergraduate student services on campus. It has also forced the programs to address expectations for different teaching styles and scheduling changes, as well as the needs and behaviors of undergraduate students. I think that the increase in undergraduate programs has been an important development in education, especially as graduates of these programs have entered LIS programs, bringing with them a high level of technology skills and often more science and technology backgrounds.

Interdisciplinarity

One of the most important and positive changes has been the growth in multiculturalism of LIS faculties and, in most cases, student bodies. Schools like ours at the University of Pittsburgh, with our LIS, IS, and Telecommunications programs, have faculty from many different countries and cultures and from a wide range of disciplines and specializations, including LIS, history, education, computer science, psychology, engineering, physics, and public policy. Students come from a diverse span of disciplines and backgrounds and from more than thirty countries around the world. While not all programs have such wide diversity, many have become much more interdisciplinary and multicultural over the years. This development has strengthened the educational experience for students and has enhanced the learning and nature of research of the faculty as well. It also has introduced challenges going far beyond the "two cultures" challenge of humanities/social science and science/engineering faculty members. The challenge has created some tensions and has demanded work to encourage people to work together, to communicate with and understand one another, and to respect others from different backgrounds. Many efforts to recruit and retain students from minority groups have been successful, but much more remains to be done. The overall effect has been very positive and has led to collaboration and partnerships not only within schools, but across schools and departments and between universities. This has strengthened our discipline and has helped to build the respect for our discipline from leaders in universities and from those in other disciplines.

Information Technology

Certainly an important change over the past few years has been the development of information technologies, often led by our own faculty and graduates. In reflecting back on some of the work we did when I was at the University of Washington's Engineering Library (with faculty in engineering to develop interest profiles and run them against the newly created NASA databases—then called Selective Dissemination of Information—or developing an "Online Commands Chart" at the National Federation of Abstracting and Indexing [now Information] Services to make it easier for people to search databases using the different Dialog, SDC or BRS services), I remember the excitement we felt about the new technologies and opportunities. While these seem primitive now, at the time they were significant steps forward with high promise for much more to come.

Information Policy and Advocacy

In working on the U.S. National Information Infrastructure Advisory Committee (NIIAC) and struggling to represent the LIS and higher education communities among a group of CEOs—Jack Valenti, Robert Kahn, Robert Johnson, and other national figures—I realized that we had a huge opportunity to make the information superhighway open to everyone and that what was crucial was to develop a set of policies to protect the values we care about so strongly. Moving from

ARPANET to NSF Net to the National Research (later and Education) Network to a democratic and open Internet and ensuring that libraries and librarians were key players was an extremely important mission. With that vision in sight and values firmly in mind, working with the NIIAC to help map the journey and advise Vice President Al Gore and Secretary of Commerce Ron Brown was a positive experience. For example, pushing for the e-rate for schools and libraries and incorporating fair and balanced policies into our reports to President Clinton were collaborative and positive experiences. Getting the attention of Vice President Gore on our work and working with him and others in the Clinton–Gore administration to develop policies and systems to improve the management of information throughout its entire life cycle without government and to begin to build true citizen-centric electronic government were major accomplishments of the LIS community. Much of that momentum has been carried forward, although there have been some serious setbacks in information policy, particularly through restrictions on access to government information and records, removal of information from federal government websites, and alarming policies, such as some components of the USA Patriot Act. Librarians have played a significant role in ensuring the role of libraries on the information superhighway, in defending civil liberties, and in speaking out for protection of values. I was personally very pleased when I stepped down after six years as chair of the board of the Center for Democracy and Technology (CDT), a not-for-profit group established ten years ago to protect civil liberties in the electronic age, to have my successor be Judith Krug, director of the Office for Intellectual Freedom of ALA. Continuing to work with her on the board has been a very positive experience and with the two of us there, CDT is hearing the voice of libraries very clearly.

Improved Information Services

Librarians have been heavily involved in developing improved information services and systems in many areas, such as digital libraries, preservation programs, software development, technical standards, international collaborative projects, education and training programs, and numerous others. Many in the corporate world and at government agencies have come to realize the knowledge and skills librarians bring to providing access to resources; organizing, managing, and preserving information; and shaping policies and plans. The value of librarians continues to be recognized, and this recognition is another important development over the past few years. It is due in part to our greater understanding of marketing what we do and to our improved ability to "tell our story."

Thoughts on the Future

So what will be important for the years ahead? Certainly, people, values, and ethics will be, along with leadership in harnessing information technologies to meet our objectives. The continuing challenges are to recruit and retain the very best people we can to be tomorrow's leaders, to replace the many individuals due to retire over the next few years, and to build the profession in preparation for the new challenges ahead. We will have to continue to fight for improvements in salaries, which are still far too low, and for the budgets needed to provide the services we know are needed.

Educating tomorrow's leaders is very, very difficult, especially within the limited time of our current programs. Ongoing curricular reform and continuing education for faculty in the discipline, in practice, and in teaching are essential. Continued focus on values and on active and real collaboration with practicing librarians and others who hire our graduates is also critical for success. We also need to find a way to build in true residency programs so that students experience working under a mentor before becoming a librarian. Certainly field experiences, internships, and paraprofessional experience are key elements of an education, but even more is needed. We in LIS education need to do more to educate and train paraprofessionals, an area we have neglected for far too long. We need to continue to strengthen our research programs and increase both funding and interdisciplinary cooperation. The quality of some of the research in our field is not as high as it should be, and we should ensure that we are educating people who know how to conduct and use research in their work and also that we do not accept or publish research that is not of high quality. The continued success of our discipline and our LIS programs depends on this improvement.

Librarians need to be even stronger as advocates for our values and for libraries and librarianship. Budget battles won't get any easier and are likely to intensify in times of constrained resources. Challenges to our values and to civil liberties may well increase, and we must be ever vigilant and ever willing to stand up for our beliefs. It is important for librarians to develop clear messages and to learn how to convey them effectively to those who can make a difference. A much more concerted effort is needed than a single day or week; we must work continuously to help people understand what we do, the value of libraries and the importance of our values. There are good workshops and other continuing education programs that can help, but more are needed. Simply posting the ALA Code of Ethics or library mission statement are not enough. We need to incorporate our values and codes of ethics into everything we do, to revisit those statements regularly and question what they mean and how we are living them.

Throughout my more than forty years in the profession, I have frequently thought about how lucky I am to be in this field at its most exciting time, whether it was the 1960s, when we worked so hard on civil rights and opening access; the 1970s, when we started to incorporate IT to make databases available; the 1980s, as we expanded services and sources; or the 1990s, as we built the Internet and the Web. As we move rapidly toward the second half of the first decade of the twenty-first century, I still believe that I am very, very fortunate to be in the most exciting profession in the world. In terms of technology, I believe that we are at a very primitive stage and that there is much more we can do to use it to really provide customized, personalized information services to each individual. I know that we can make libraries much better collectors and preservers of our culture and certainly more hospitable places for people to want to visit. Why, I keep wondering, haven't we gotten bookstores to join forces with libraries in one location, with a café or tea room, yes, but also perhaps with a movie theater? People could borrow materials from the library and participate in story hours or senior programs, go into the bookstore to buy a copy of materials they want to own, and go see a new movie by a director they just read about. There are so many possibilities for the library as place, as well as information provider. It is these exciting possibilities and the opportunity to help educate our future colleagues that make me thankful every day I am in this field. I can't wait to see what comes next.

Suggested Readings

American Library Association. "Report of the Core Values Task Force II: ALA Conference 2004." http://www.ala.org/ala/oif/statementspols/corevaluesstatement/core values.htm.

———. "Report of the Core Values Task Force II: 2004 ALA Midwinter Meeting." http://www.ala.org/ala/ourassociation/governanceb/council/councilagendas/mw2004agendas/CD7.doc (January 2004).

Capurro, Rafael. "Foundations of Information Science Review and Perspectives." Available at http://www.capurro.de/tampere91.htm. Originally published as "What Is Information Science For? A Philosophical Reflection," pp. 82–98 in *Conceptions of Library and Information Science: Historical, Empirical and Theoretical Perspectives*, ed. Pertti Vakkari and Blaise Cronin. London: Taylor Graham, 1992.

Carter, Stephen L. *Integrity.* New York: HarperCollins, 1996.

Dalai Lama. *Ethics for the New Millennium.* New York: Riverhead Books, 1999.

Dole, Wanda V., and Jitka M. Hurych. "Values for Librarians in the Information Age." *Journal of Information Ethics* 10, no. 2 (Fall 2001): 38–50.

Koehler, Wallace. "Professional Values and Ethics as Defined by 'The LIS Discipline.'" *Journal of Education for Library and Information Science* 44, no. 2 (Spring 2003): 99–110.

Lencioni, Patrick M. "Make Your Values Mean Something." *Harvard Business Review* 80, no. 7 (July 2002): 113–117.

Paul, Richard, and Linda Elder. *The Miniature Guide to Understanding the Foundations of Ethical Reasoning.* Dillon Beach, Calif.: Foundation for Critical Thinking, 2003.

Ranganathan, S. R. *Library Book Selection.* New Delhi: Indian Library Association, 1952. Quoted in Gorman, G. E., and B. R. Howes, *Collection Development for Libraries* (London; New York: Bowker-Saur; Wagga Wagga, New South Wales: Centre for Information Studies, Riverina-Murray Institute of Higher Education, 1989).

Serving Young Adults in Libraries: A Professional Life's Work

MARY K. CHELTON

I HAVE OFTEN DESCRIBED MYSELF as a many-layered onion with young adult (YA) services as the solid core of my professional being. I came about this naturally. When I was a teenager, I found the YA department in the Enoch Pratt Free Library in Baltimore and felt I had died and gone to heaven. I was treated like royalty, read all kinds of books I would never have sought otherwise, for the sole reason that I was flattered that Anna Gallagher, the Central YA Librarian, suggested them to me. At some point during adolescence, as a result of my encounters with her and other Pratt librarians, I realized that I did not need to get married or become a teacher or nurse or secretary—the only options that a Catholic school girl felt were open to her then. I could become like these women whom I admired and be a librarian. I've never regretted it, feeling always that I have followed in great footsteps, with an eye toward who would follow in mine. Having known personally what their attention to a lonely, bookish kid meant, I vowed to pass that attention and affection on to other young people, and my passion for the work on to other librarians.

This passion for passing on the work was reinforced by a small exchange with Pauline Winnick in the 1970s. Pauline then worked for the federal department of education's library services office in Washington, D.C. I told her in passing, with some excitement that I expected to be shared, that I had just gotten a YA position in the Prince George's County (Maryland) Memorial Library. Her immediate response was, "And who are you training to replace you?" which completely annoyed me at the time. Hell, I had not been in the new job six months yet! It is probably to this day one of the three most important things anyone ever said to me, and I will never forget it.

Someone asked me several years ago what I wanted, and I said, "immortality."

I did not mean this in any spiritual sense, but only in the sense that I wanted people to know that I had been here and cared passionately about what I did, enough to leave a record of my thoughts and activities for others. This is why I write and have encouraged others to write, and I enjoy watching a flourishing professional literature on services to young adults emerge, in large part because of the work Dorothy Broderick and I did on *Voice of Youth Advocates* (*VOYA*) magazine. Dorothy and I were hallway and back of the room observers to a big fight between the children's and YA divisions of ALA in the 1970s, where the Young Adult Services Division (YASD, now YALSA) was threatening to count the pages allotted in their shared journal, *Top of the News* (*TON*), if the editors did not pay more attention to YA interests. Fortunately for Dorothy and me, one of the *TON* editors was overheard to remark, "*They* don't have anything to say." We not only got mad; we got even, which is how *VOYA* was conceived. We felt strongly that a service without a voice of its own could not survive, especially as a subcategory of children's services. It just did not make developmental sense. It is interesting to watch the most brilliant of our new writers and mentees, Patrick Jones, continue the process by inviting new, innovative YA librarians to co-author books with him today.

While both Dorothy and I were probably destined to become professional writers—she long before I—I'm not sure that snarky remark alone would have made us start *VOYA* if it had not been for the example set by Carol Starr. Carol, who was the YA Coordinator in Contra Costa County's library system in California then, started something in the early 1960s called the *Young Adult Alternative Newsletter,* when I was the system consultant for YA Services in the Westchester Library System outside New York City. It was so helpful, practical, iconoclastic, and at the same time issue oriented that it succeeded in uniting a community of us, from coast to coast, who cared about the age group. We were largely the third generation of administrative YA specialists in large public library systems, and Carol's energy and ultimately her election to the YASD presidency, launched many of us who are now the new crop of "senior citizen" YA specialists mentoring and watching the fourth and fifth generations go to it. Ironically, Carol and I both worked for Julia Losinski in the Prince George's County Memorial Library System in Maryland at different times under the same branch librarian, Ed Talbert. While a quiet, determined, handsome, and somewhat formal man, I like to think he recognized talent when it came his way, and we were both very grateful for his support and mentorship while soaking up Losinski's training and service philosophy, which Ed reinforced in an ideal staff-line administrative relationship. I don't know if he did this for Carol, but like all my best line administrators, he managed to keep me from shooting myself in the foot, which seems to be a major YA librarian personality failing.

Not only did Carol get me into ALA via YASD, she wrote a history of the division so we would have some idea of where we came from, and spent a lot of time first learning and then explaining ALA structure to me, so that, when I ran for office myself, I had a lot of background. What she didn't teach me, I learned during long lunches with Lillian Gerhardt, then the editor of *School Library Journal* (and subsequently a Grolier Award winner herself) in New York City during my time at Westchester. I got a great deal of organizational experience from a term on Council, being a division president and being on various ALA and divisional committees. The best experience, though, came from being YASD's president-elect at the time ALA basically federated itself through a change in its dues structure. I sat with ten other people in the other divisions and made friends across the association while trying to figure out how to save a small division from going under from the cost of maintaining itself. This was also during Evelyn Shaevel's tenure as executive director of YASD, to which she brought a good brain, a sense of fun and commitment to the age group, an impressive professional wardrobe, and years of listening to her parents discuss temple politics at home, all of which helped her immensely at ALA headquarters. The "shared staffing" arrangement she devised with Anne Weeks saved the division during that difficult time, since most public library YA people were not very numerous and entry-level librarians too poor to shell out the kind of dues the division needed for survival. YA school librarians also supported the American Association of School Librarians, so additional support for YASD made them pay two sets of dues.

The other unique political and organizational experience I had was in becoming, by virtue of my relationship with Dorothy, an "associate member" of the group we affectionately call the "Moon Mafia." These were the friends of Eric and Ilse Moon, most of whom occupied the "back bench" at Council while I was on it. I agreed with their politics instinctively, and learned to understand savvy professional commitment that bright people could make seem like play. When Eric Moon was ALA president, he put me on his National Information Policy Committee at a time when I had given national information policy no thought whatsoever and faced a steep learning curve, but we did manage to come up with a document despite the distractions of ALA's internal censorship controversy over defense of a racist speaker in a film ostensibly produced to make people think about censorship and free speech.

The only reason I have listed these ALA experiences is because I find it very frustrating that other YA librarians cannot, or will not, get them. Most people joining YALSA want to be on the Best Books for Young Adults Committee or,

as a second choice, one of the other selection committees. One notable YA librarian, who shall remain nameless, got involved in the association through being on
that committee and then ran for the YALSA board, only to find herself stultified
at board meetings and thinking about resigning. A lot of YA people have some
sort of Peter Pan mentality, or they can't stand to be bored for very long. I fight
that tendency in myself always.

A lot of the hard work of organizations is tedious and frustrating, but possi-
bly because of the financial cost of ALA participation, many contemporary YA
librarians do not want to do something strange outside the protective cocoon; as
a result, the YA perspective and voice is often lost. I educated my ALA Professional Ethics Committee colleagues about the miserable practices in many public
libraries regarding teenagers, something they would not have heard had I not been
there. Of course, this only happened during endless meetings about interpretations of the ALA Statement on Professional Ethics. I once learned, after several
years of working and making friends in the Public Library Association (PLA) of
ALA, about a camp for teenager library pages the PLA was considering but had
been blown off by YALSA. I went to YALSA (where I had not only once served
as president, but still had many professional friends) to ask about it, only to be
told, "Well, you haven't been active in this division for a long time . . ." In other
words, we only recognize others in the same ghetto. My experience in ALA and
with the Moon folks enlarged my professional worldview considerably, to the
point that I winced when confronted recently by a well-meaning but naïve librarian who might want a Ph.D. but doesn't want to study or teach anything other
than the thing they already know, usually children's or adolescent literature.

If I had taken the ghetto mentality course of the diehard specialist, I never
would have initiated the *Bare Bones Young Adult Services* monograph. By that time, I
had a position in Montgomery County, Maryland, where I was an Adult/Young
Adult Coordinator, and Ted Balcom, who was wonderfully ignorant of my YA
background, asked me to keynote a workshop on reader's advisory services for
adults. He and I also planned the structure of the overall PLA workshop, which
included role playing exercises. During those exercises, I watched librarian after
librarian role play YA reader's advisory scenarios, and the idea to write a manual
for people who worked with teenagers in public libraries but did not consider
themselves specialists. The first edition sold 6,000 copies, some sort of ALA publishing record, and despite the initial resistance when I suggested it to the children's people, I notice there is a children's services counterpart in print now.

I was an Enoch Pratt Free Library (Maryland) scholarship winner to library
school (yes, urban libraries had money then) where I actually had Margaret Alex-
ander Edwards as my teacher for young adult literature, after having been trained

as a "pre-professional" by her successors in that library. She was predictably wonderful, and I subsequently had the Bay Area YA Librarians group (BAYA) invite her to speak at a meeting in San Francisco a decade later when she was promoting a reprint or revised edition of her book *The Fair Garden and the Swarm of Beasts: The Library and the Young Adult.* BAYA members were torn because a big antiwar protest was being held outside the library and many wanted to participate themselves. In deference to Edwards, though, the bulk of them stayed, and I still remember a mesmerizing book talk on *Wuthering Heights* in a Texas twang and a background of antiwar chanting outside.

As important as she was, Edwards was only one of many Grolier Award winners I either worked for or came to know personally through work in ALA. Others included her successor YA coordinator at Enoch Pratt, Sara Siebert, the inimitable Anne Izard, Children's Services Consultant for most of my time at the Westchester Library System in New York, and Julia Losinski, the YA Services Coordinator in Prince George's County Memorial Library. I used to sit in Julia's office and read her award hanging framed on the wall while waiting for her to get off the phone or for meetings to begin. To me, that award always meant the personification of superb library services for young adults, which is why I organized the effort behind Mike Printz receiving it. Of all of us, he was the most incredible, I think, and he still remains in memory, the best librarian—and the best YA librarian—I ever knew. I first met him on a street corner in Los Angeles after a YASD preconference to decide the "best of the best" books in a ten-year retrospective. I had heard about him from the late Bill Morris, HarperCollins much beloved vice president of juvenile book marketing, but we had never met until then. Amid the winos and homeless of downtown L.A., we ranted on that corner about favorite books that had not made the list, and became friends. To say that Mike was a revelation is a vast understatement.

First of all, Mike was a school librarian for his entire career, and being Enoch Pratt and Edwards molded, I was never quite sure about those people, seeing them merely as a means to get into schools to do book talks and little more. Well, Mike still holds the record for being one of the best book people I have ever known, but he also adored kids and was an educator down to his toenails. I once agreed to write something on services evaluation, and since I had learned that many secondary school librarians did indeed consider themselves to be YA librarians under a different name, I called him up to ask about services objectives to make sure I was not missing anything important. I gave him a couple of days to get back to me, and without missing a beat on the phone, he said he didn't need a couple of days and then proceeded to reel off an incredible laundry list of what YA services are all about. I was one of many who absolutely adored him, but I am also one who will never forgive YALSA the irony of naming an award after him that, by definition, does not include books published for adults and of interest to young adults. He paid the way for kids from his high school in Topeka, Kansas, to come to YASD Best Books Committee meetings to make that very point at one of the New York City ALA conferences. History gets warped regularly in ALA's short memory, but this particular warp is more annoying than most.

Thanks to being a "good girl" from Catholic schools, I did not know how to do anything but please nuns and nun surrogates in the workplace. I have Dick Moses (founder of High John Library) to thank for the overdue process of learning how to question the status quo, which, in retrospect, is probably in a YA librarian's genetic makeup. Luckily our time at Enoch Pratt crossed, and I was parroting some conventional wisdom about displaying books at a training meeting when he challenged me—much more politely than I have done to others since, by the way—realizing that you are a fool is a great wake-up opportunity. Ultimately, this led to my challenging a lot of things taken for granted by Edwards and her successors at Pratt. Her autocratic style of book talk training terrified some good library trainees who left YA services rather than submit to it, and I learned how to be both more flexible and more understanding about introverts who are better with kids one-on-one and not in love with the sound of their own voices, like yours truly. I also learned that information-seeking and serving the kids doing it was not something easily relegated to the scorn Edwards gave it, and now realize that the new research on boys and reading serves to underscore the importance of information books (as opposed to fiction and memoirs) and the appeal of computers. Since most kids come into public libraries because of school assignments (imposed queries), giving them good reference service and information literacy instruction is the only way to win their trust to do any reading promotion, which Edwards equated with YA services. You cannot have a society that insists on mandatory schooling and ignore the school-related needs of adolescents. I am disheartened, however, about the dichotomy over the instructional role that has emerged in YA services between school and public libraries.

It was a great shock to me when I realized that I did not want to be a YA coordinator all my working life. This specialty position was long considered the epitome of the YA career ladder for my generation, although Carol Starr herself once said to me that we would both be library directors one day, which she was, but I was not. I found that I liked setting up training and creating a cohesive community of librarians who could learn from one another, but the idea of maintaining all of it for twenty years bored me silly. I was also annoyed that most LIS academics never seemed to be doing any research on anything I cared about, so after several false starts, I got a Ph.D. and researched service interactions between adults and adolescents in library setting. It is sometimes lonely, not only because of the love–hate relationship most practitioners have with library schools, but also because most of the other YA people with Ph.D.s are either from school libraries and interested in information literacy instruction or they come from public libraries and study adolescent literature instead of services. I find this to be a mistake, partly because new research on boys and reading is pointing out that the emphasis by teachers and librarians on literature and the narrative experience is actually creating disincentives for boys to read. This also keeps them from recognizing boys who are readers, just not readers that mostly female librarians recognize.

Despite all my academic credentials and lofty position title, I often feel like the oldest living YA librarian and wonder whether this is a good thing or a bad thing. Being able to mentor people is very rewarding, and learning about the creativity of those coming behind me in my work on the Excellence in Library Services for Young Adults monographs was inspiring. On the other hand, trying to understand or like graphic novels in my sixties is killing me, even when I recognize that that is where the YA reader action is now, not with the Printz Award titles. Reading YA fiction for pleasure personally is long gone; they are all work now. Figuring out what to write and how to structure training for people who need to know how to interact with adolescents in libraries regardless of position title remains an interesting challenge. Suggesting YA-related masters research to students looking for research ideas gets a lot of topics examined that would otherwise go begging. This remains one of the best reasons for getting myself credentialed to be a fulltime library educator. Watching the information science people discover the K-12 audience has been interesting, although I think many of them still lack understanding of developmental realities and use school captive audiences too much. Seeing YALSA stabilize finances through endorsements for Teen Read Week has been nice, despite a deplorable tendency that makes ALA seem to be for sale to the highest commercial bidder these days.

Overall, though, I have been very lucky in my choice of careers and in the specialty I loved. So many kids are raising themselves these days that I like to think that librarians can make a difference in their lives, and I hope that I have.

Libraries: The Best Public Value

GINNIE COOPER

L IBRARIES ARE THE BEST public value. People connect with information and ideas at libraries. Libraries help people make these connections in a variety of ways using books, information that people want and need, the Internet, special programs for children and adults, buildings that inspire community pride, and more. This has been the role of libraries for more than a century. In the future, connecting people with ideas will continue to be what is done at libraries. How libraries do this has changed through time. In fact, how people connect with ideas is changing everyday at libraries everywhere.

Public libraries are funded locally, with most funding coming from local taxes; relatively little federal and state funds help to pay for library services. Although public libraries are funded and governed locally, public libraries have much in common. Nearly all public libraries offer books for borrowing, serve children, offer interlibrary loans, help people find information, and in many other ways are similar. Libraries are collaborative institutions; librarians learn from each other. Library staff learns from one another through professional associations, conferences, and other common settings.

Libraries also have in common being viewed favorably by most people. In part, this comes from the transfer of good will and expectations from one library to another. Many people value and support libraries today because of their experiences with libraries in their past.

In addition, libraries face similar challenges. Most notably, libraries face the challenge of adapting and changing because the world around us is changing. We don't control the future, or know exactly what is ahead. Here are some ideas that I believe are likely to affect libraries.

In the next decade, workers 55–64 years old will be retiring in great numbers. This group of retirees is projected to include one-third of those involved in education, including librarians and teachers. We are already seeing this in the library profession. Currently, for each new master's degree awarded in library science, two librarians are retiring. At the same time, as many education professionals are ending their work lives, many more beyond just replacements will be needed. Worldwide population projections suggest that twice as many new teachers and librarians will be needed.

Labor shortages are increasing in nearly every area, including libraries. In order to cope with these shortages, the number of temporary employment agencies is increasing. There are new trends emerging in how people work. Employers offer part-time jobs to attract more workers. Older workers "retire" but continue to work. Gone is the time when workers assumed their first employer would be their workplace for life. Young people want flexibility and are demanding it, either from one job or by going from job to job.

Available jobs are changing in other ways, too. More and more people will work in technology. Of the ten fastest growing jobs, eight are in technology; the remaining two are in health care. This will be the environment in which libraries will seek new workers.

Of course, libraries will be seeking technology workers, too. Technology has changed the way libraries connect people with ideas, and there is every indication the changes in the future will be even greater. Sixty-five percent of people in the United States have cell phones. This number continues to increase, and is already greater in other countries, for example, Finland and Israel. In 2003, more than 50 percent of the population engaged in e-commerce, and this number continues to increase. About 20 percent of homes now have broadband Internet access, and this number will increase rapidly as the service becomes more affordable. By 2005, two-thirds of homes will be Internet-connected. As use of computers increases, users want computers that are faster and can do more. My ninety-one-year-old mother, for example, says she thinks the new computer we recently bought for her isn't fast enough!

Another change is coming—with even greater impact on the way we live and work. Pervasive computing, or machines talking to machines, is on the rise. Today, refrigerators are able to order groceries and cars are getting recall notices and scheduling service. Human workers will be needed less often for these tasks, and telephone "help desks" will become less common.

These and other changes are already finding a place in libraries. With the increasing number of workers retiring and fewer people available to fill these vacancies, libraries will change even more. Libraries will lead the way neither in researching nor in adopting new technology, but libraries will adapt developing technology.

Radio-frequency Identification Chips (RFID) is one example. Wal-Mart led the way with bar codes—now so much a part of how libraries keep track of books and borrowers. Wal-Mart now says it will require radio-frequency identification (RFID) chips in all products at its distribution centers by January 2005. This technology is already finding a place at libraries. At Brooklyn Public Library, we expect to have this technology in place in the next five to eight years. We look forward to the RFID tags that will store additional information, and to the ability to locate and track material.

Many libraries now use automated telephone systems. Voice recognition systems are rapidly becoming much more sophisticated. Though I hate most voice-mail menus, recently I have been impressed with systems that sound like real people and allow me to "say" my question rather than asking that I "press 1 for . . . or 2 for . . ."

With even greater potential for changing lives would be success in the long search for cheaper power. The dream is of a universal transformer that can take any fuel source and make it useable, bringing down the cost of power. This "Holy Grail" has long been predicted and may actually come to pass.

Wi-Fi access, the ability to access the Internet without wires, is my personal favorite. In the last few years, this new technology has appeared everywhere: Paris Metro Stations, airports, coffee shops, even my apartment. We access the Internet everywhere! Phones, computers, PDAs, and other specialty devices allow pervasive computing for people. Wi-fi antennas are less expensive and cover larger areas, and use of wi-fi will increase as the cost decreases.

In New York City, wi-fi is available at Manhattan's Bryant Park, behind the New York Public Library, and at the new entrance plaza of the Brooklyn Museum of Art. Within the next decade, wireless technology will make us "globally" wired. In India, Internet-enabled computers are selling for $150, making the technology available to many more. India's officials are planning to put antennas on public buses. If you've been to India, you know that buses are everywhere, carrying chickens, goats, people, and more! These traveling antennas will bring wireless access throughout India.

By 2010, we will be talking conversationally to realistic, life-size images to do commerce and other kinds of interactions. Imagine giving a medical history to such a device instead of filling out forms. All this and more will result in "Tele Living," living through the intelligent Internet.

What will all this mean to libraries? Imagine a world where libraries deal with staffing challenges through artificial, intelligent, animated images. This would allow scarce staff to be available for work that requires a human touch, such as reading to children or helping a library user find information.

I have suggested some factors that will affect the future of libraries. I'm sure I have gotten some things completely wrong. After all, Bill Gates initially thought the Internet would not be an important factor in computing. But likely we, and Mr. Gates, can count on change in our future!

Two things are certain about the future, easing my concern about what our world will become. First, the future arrives gradually, not all at once, and it arrives first in one place then in others. We see our future coming, sometimes several years in advance. Second, we don't control the future—no one does! In libraries, we do not control the research or development of technology that will affect us. But if we are skilled, we can understand and anticipate the changes that are inevitable. .

In the present, the most valuable asset of libraries is favorable public opinion. We rely on this asset, and use it for our support. Often we hear people say, "Oh, I love the library!" even if they *never* come into the library or use it in any way. We who care about libraries need to tend this most valuable asset, and use it wisely. In the political atmosphere in which libraries are funded and operate, we will use favorable public opinion to successfully navigate the present and into the future.

Librarians must examine the needs of the library users and communities that they serve. What are the community's problems and issues? What appropriate role can the library play in addressing these priorities? Often the best way to identify specific priorities is to *listen* to politicians and other decision makers. They are successful because they accurately voice their constituents' concerns. And their constituents are potential library users.

Issues will differ among communities; the following are examples of common priorities: business and economic growth; crime reductions and safety; building a sense of community; concern with specific populations, such as children, senior citizens, ethnic groups, or others.

As libraries are seen to respond to such priorities, they will be viewed as valuable to their communities. Mark H. Moore, author of *Creating Public Value: Strategic Management in Government*, talks about what public managers need to do in order to create public value as a *strategic triangle*. Here are the components of Moore's strategic triangle:

I. Identify the mission or purpose of the public organization, stated in terms of response to important local priorities and public values. We need to see libraries in terms of the particular distinctive competencies and strategically important assets we control. Some we can identify easily like information finding, working with kids, supporting the work of schools. Others are less commonly identified as library assets like buildings, often a presence in every neighborhood; space for meetings; and the asset of favorable public opinion. To the extent that people do not understand what libraries do, we are in trouble. Publicly funded libraries must do what contemporary politics require. And this leads to the second part of the strategic triangle.

II. Manage upward, toward politics, to be sure the mission of the organization has legitimacy and will have support. Will the library's mission and the services provided by libraries be understood and welcomed by decision makers in our communities, and supported financially? Public library advocates must be skilled in congruity. In other words, we must make clear the connection between public/political priorities and what we do. Libraries will only be funded to the degree they are understood to be carrying out what society, specifically those who control the funding, understand to be the community's needs. It is critical to address today's needs, not what might have been of value in the past. What libraries do must make sense to those who make decisions; only then will libraries be supported and thrive.

III. Manage downward, improving the organization's capabilities for achieving the desired purposes. The next step? Making libraries functionally able to provide what our communities need. This is often the most difficult step. The strong lure to continue services long provided is difficult, sometimes impossible, to overcome. There are library services that respond to common community priorities. Tailoring programs and services for specific neighborhoods we serve is one step. Working with schools, children, and seniors is another response to priorities in some communities. Libraries also offer homework help, and job and business information.

Though this work within libraries is sometimes the most difficult, we are getting smarter and more strategic about how libraries work. We have no choice! In this time of staffing challenges, technological changes, limited funding, and more, we need to examine how our institutions operate and then reorganize.

We must deal with all three elements of Moore's strategic triangle for libraries to successfully create value for the public we serve. Libraries must be seen as effective educational and cultural tools for the community, responding to important problems and issues. Libraries must be more than an abstract "good thing."

Libraries have so much to offer. More than any other publicly supported institution, libraries are places of learning and equity. Libraries should be understood to be part of how critical community issues will be addressed so everyone will realize libraries truly are the best public value!

A Virtuous Profession

LEIGH S. ESTABROOK

SEVENTY-TWO-YEAR-OLD South African playwright Athol Fugard spoke recently of the fear of being unneeded, unwanted and useless—fears many of us share as we near the end of our work lives. Those of us who have been librarians or helped educate librarians may indeed feel that way about ourselves—but we know that our work is needed, wanted and useful. Librarianship is a practice in philosopher Alasdair MacIntyre's sense—a worthwhile human social activity that requires us to act with virtue, that is, with courage, justice, and honesty.

Our library users deeply need us to provide alternative and competing points of view. We are witnessing increasing media consolidation and cross-ownership of media, so our users hear fewer voices in their normal course of television watching and newspaper reading. We experience the growing range of Clear Channel radio with a concomitant loss of local programming and local information. We are ordered by the Department of Justice to destroy nonclassified government documents that are useful to our fellow citizens. We are needed to influence and shape public information policy. We are needed to create information resources that the market will not create. We are needed to preserve our culture. In the process, we are called upon to act ethically ourselves.

MacIntyre's discussion of these matters can help us think about the practice of librarianship and our role within it, but to do so requires an initial explanation of his concepts. His book *After Virtue* seeks to reconcile the different definitions of virtue and the virtues from Aristotle to modern times, as illustrated by authors as different as Jane Austen and Benjamin Franklin. To do so, he gives a particular definition to the notion of a practice and to what he calls its internal and external goods:

By a "practice" I am going to mean any coherent and complex form of socially established cooperative human activity through which goods internal to that form of activity are realized in the course of trying to achieve those standards of excellence which are appropriate to, and partially definitive of, that form of activity, with the result that human powers to achieve excellence, and human conceptions of the ends and goods involved, are systematically extended. (p. 187)

When achieved, "external goods . . . are always some individual's property and possession" (p. 190). These may include power, fame, money—goods associated with the individual, not with the community. The more one person has of these goods, the less likely another may have them as our society is currently constructed. Librarians' striving for the external goods of professional status appears for most of us to be a good thing: recognition for the value of our work, better pay, higher respect for our activities.

Practice is the doing of some work or task, but as MacIntyre defines it, it involves only certain kinds of tasks: those that involve a worthwhile social goal. So he would say that circulating books is not a practice, but librarianship—including making books accessible and findable, reference, readers' advisory services, and the complex pieces of work that may ultimately lead to the circulation of a book—is a practice. Institutions are not practices, although practices are often carried on within institutions.

Internal goods are fundamentally different from and stand in contrast to external goods. Specific to a practice, they "are indeed the outcome of competition to excel, but it is characteristic of them that their achievement is a good for the whole community who participate in the practice" (p. 190f.). Since he believes the internal goods of practice require the human practice of truthfulness, justice, and courage, it follows that achievement of external goods and internal goods may well be contradictory. Moreover, and of particular importance as I seek to apply these notions to librarianship, "without justice, courage and truthfulness, practices could not resist the corrupting power of institutions" (p. 194).

When I consider the practice of librarianship, MacIntyre provides helpful insight into struggles in the field that have existed for many decades and continue to challenge us. Let me offer two examples: our striving for professional status and our endless quest to defend intellectual freedom. He also helps to reveal some of the reasons that this practice of librarianship can be so rewarding and sustaining as a human endeavor. I'll begin with the struggles.

Striving for professional status is a community effort, as the efforts of the American Library Association and other professional groups show. It also involves individual behavior—seeking external goods such as higher salaries, respect, and greater autonomy in the workplace. I cannot quarrel with the value and necessity of obtaining them. (I frequently teach people the art of salary negotiations.) Yet we know from a host of research and from our own experience that professional striving—absent the virtue of justice—can be contradictory to the internal values of librarianship. We know, for example, that professional striving can lead to practitioners referring away to others, rather than serving, those clients who seem less desirable—those who are deemed lower in status as judged by superficial characteristics such as race, age, or gender. Before dismissing this assertion, consider the hierarchy of librarianship that places members of ARL libraries in a higher status than community college librarians. And consider the relative status granted to us by the age groups with which we work, or the wealth of our communities. It is this striving that leads to the tensions between paraprofessionals and professionals in many libraries, even when such tension is dysfunctional to our accomplishing the tasks of the library. It is this striving that has often set librarians outside the labor movement.

If our striving for external goods contradicts the fundamental values of librarianship, each of our quests to be just, truthful, and courageous becomes impossible. My life and the lives of friends and colleagues are filled with the struggle between wanting those external goods and desiring to act virtuously. As librarians, we are called to treat all users equally and with justice; to tell the truth through the variety, balance, and choices of information we provide; and to act with courage, since the values we hold are often challenged by individuals, by governments, and even within the institutions in which we work. For example, the practice of librarianship is bound up with a commitment to intellectual freedom—again a goal fostered by our professional associations but practiced by individuals in concert with others. It has been individual courage and commitment to justice that day by day, library by library, result in the availability of important but controversial books. It is the person, not the association, who is confronted with law enforcement officers asking for information about a user. It is the person, with courage and justice and aligned with the philosophy of librarianship, who faces the school board to defend the library's acquisition of a questioned title.

MacIntyre stresses that practitioners have relationships to one another that are defined by the mission of the practice and by the virtues of the people in that practice. Perhaps that was my earliest indication of the nature of librarianship—the qualities of the people I met and their values exercised in collaboration. Beginning with early discussions in Ken Kister's class on intellectual freedom, through the Rutgers Pre-conference on Women in the 1970s, and throughout thirty years of argument, discussion, and mutual learning with faculty, colleagues, and students—I have been taught that the strength of this practice depends on the way that we accompany one another. That sense of accompaniment is essential to our attaining the ideals of our virtuous profession. And librarianship's continuous commitment to the goal of access in all its implications is the ideal that we hold in common.

Librarianship allows us to be whole people, to act ethically ourselves and to seek the common good. But librarianship also requires us to submit to the community of librarianship and the mission of the practice our personal desires and even perhaps our personal beliefs of what justice, truth, and courage involve and not all in the field see the matter in the same way. My students face potential conflict between person and role each semester. One year, three students who described themselves as fundamentalist Christians came to me to complain about how another instructor talked about the efforts of some fundamentalist Christian groups to eliminate materials from a library. They regarded these examples as illustrative of the instructor's prejudice against fundamentalists and saw the examples as creating a hostile environment. I explained to the students that they had a right to express their views in the classroom and to be treated with respect, but that they also had to realize that the professor had offered a real example.

When I have raised with students the question of contradictions between personal beliefs and the tenets of librarianship, I have found that some have faced difficult decisions about whether they can practice as librarians. If they feel that they cannot join in a commitment to free and open access to materials, can they practice librarianship in any but certain restricted settings? I have had parents in class who say they want all Internet terminals filtered—that they fear for their children and therefore think that they must fear for the children of their users. Do they practice librarianship if they are willing to undermine its core values?

LIS education has been taken to task for not inculcating values into our students. We do, but it is extraordinarily difficult to come to terms with cases like these. We need to find ways to respect the individual values of our students and colleagues and at the same time insist on the necessity of librarians' commitment to practicing with justice, truth, and courage—without imposing our own prejudices. That is extremely difficult, but it is the struggle of our history, and it will continue.

A friend once commented that she did not understand how I could be a librarian when she found me so angry toward the profession—this, after listening to me complain about a situation in which I thought some librarians had been too complacent and cowardly. And I do get angry. When librarians bow to the chilling effect of the DMCA and do not assert Fair Use rights for matters as yet unsettled in law, we are not taking risks to fight for access. When we know that there is information that might be useful to gay teenagers but do not acquire it or shelve it in the young adult section because we fear community reaction—or because we do not ourselves like those materials—we are not being courageous, nor are we being just. I am angry because I am disappointed. I am disappointed even when I realize that the library as an institution is governed by a lay board or is responding to the demands of a wider community. *Corruptio optimi pessima* is the classic maxim: "the corruption of the best is the worst of all."

Our practice is often corrupted, our fundamental goals are often compromised, by the institutionalization of our work. Librarians require collections, staff, and a host of interlocking activities necessary for libraries to provide access to materials. Our institutions are funded by and governed by communities with their own expectations and standards. Increasingly we also find libraries the subject of governmental control and regulation, including copyright and communications law and a host of directives following the events of September 11, 2001. We can understand then MacIntyre's point that "without justice, courage and truthfulness, practices could not resist the corrupting power of institutions" (p. 194). We see the ongoing struggle of any librarian between his or her person and the role within an institution.

We are also corrupted or compromised by our own desires for external goods—not surprisingly. I want to send my children to decent schools. I need to have them covered by health insurance. Jobs are not plentiful, and it would be rash in many cases to oppose my board or to expose a search warrant. But the choices are rarely so simple, and we can make great differences—by educating our users and boards, by working together to change the regulations of the Patriot Act, and by other actions that promote the remarkable and important mission of the field. We can also accompany one another.

I mentioned accompaniment earlier. The word is also used by those of us who have worked with the dispossessed and politically vulnerable in Latin America, and in that case, accompaniment includes the important notion that people from the rich and powerful nations should accompany those whose wealth and power have been taken away by the actions of those wealthier countries. This usage best suggests what I think needs to be done if we are to sustain our profession virtuously.

Those of us who have attained relative wealth and power in this field—the authors in this book, for example—must accompany those who have not. It is a painfully difficult decision for the mother of young children to risk her job by standing up against the school board or to risk prison by violating the gag rule of the USA Patriot Act to inform a patron that the FBI has requested his records. My children are grown, and the risk for me would be minimal by comparison. I

48 LEIGH S. ESTABROOK

could even retire, and those paychecks would keep coming, even while I was in prison. Those of us who are older and established and can afford the risks should be accompanying those for whom the risks are much greater. Jeanette Rankin, the only Congressperson to vote against the United States' entry into both World War I and II, once said, "If I had my life to live over, I would do it all again, but this time I would be nastier."

Reference

MacIntyre, Alasdair C. *After Virtue*. 2nd ed. South Bend, Ind.: University of Notre Dame Press, 1984.

Librarians: Our Reach Is Global and Our Touch Is Local

BARBARA J. FORD

"Be the change you want to see in the world."

—GHANDI

BEING A LIBRARIAN has shaped my life, values, goals, and relationships. I am proud to be part of a profession that has and will lead in shaping how people find and evaluate the information they need to learn, grow, and improve their lives. People are the basis of all we do and are what make library programs sustainable and effective. As change agents, we should identify the best of what is today and use that information to pursue opportunities for what the future can be as we work for positive change. As I reflect on librarianship, there are a number of approaches that have enriched my life and work.

Think Global

The library profession is energized by the expanding interest of librarians in global issues. As global citizens, we share responsibility in creating a better, more just and equitable world. We have the power to make important changes by an activism demonstrated through library programs and services and as part of larger movements. We must cultivate a universal responsibility for one another and act on that responsibility. Thinking beyond one's own culture and country can lead to innovative ideas. Solutions developed in one part of the world can be adapted for use in other places. Global contexts can lead to global solutions that help libraries and people move into the future in inventive ways. How we continue to expand our global reach is one of the ongoing opportunities and challenges for all librarians.

In each of my positions in academic, public, medical, and special libraries, I have been able to find global aspects in my work. During my year as president of the American Library Association, 1997–1998, we focused on the global reach and local touch of libraries. A collaborative process generated several strategies to extend the boundaries of library service.

Celebrate diversity. Reach out to community or campus groups reflecting other cultures and countries, and celebrate that diversity with speakers, exhibits, films, and special performances. Plan programs, displays, and fairs for international holidays, and United Nations and world commemorative days. Sponsor a series of lectures or presentations on different countries or world regions. Invite returned Peace Corps volunteers, Fulbright Scholars, or others with international experience to speak.

Expand and diversify your library's services and collection of multicultural and multilingual materials. Add United Nations materials and publications to your collection. Include materials on language learning. Provide multilingual online catalogs. Host reading groups with an international focus.

Develop an international dimension to library services. Hold staff seminars on understanding students and library users from other cultures. Make a list of staff who speak other languages and are available to assist in translation. Provide multilingual tours of libraries. Hold workshops for staff on how to incorporate stories, ideas, and music from various cultures in programming.

Use the Internet to connect to other cultures. Provide lists of international libraries, United Nations, and other web sites that promote learning about other countries, cultures, international travel, and global cooperation. Bookmark Internet sites of newspapers from various countries that will help promote libraries to immigrants and businesses hoping to expand overseas. Design interactive web-based materials and training courses to encourage and foster diversity.

Promote public awareness of global resources at your library during special library weeks and every week. Provide monthly suggestions of multicultural celebrations and programs. Look for opportunities to partner with other nonprofit organizations to increase global awareness between libraries and expand the knowledge of the role libraries play in global settings.

Learn more about global information issues such as copyright, and how they affect libraries around the world. Become a member of association divisions and sections with a special focus on international issues, such as preservation. Take advantage of the membership and newsletters of UNESCO's Network of Associated Libraries and indicate which of the UNESCO themes (cultural development, peace, cultural dialogue, status of women, environment, youth, human rights, and literacy campaigns) you want to support.

Connect with libraries and librarians in other countries. If your city has a Sister City program, seek sponsorship for an exchange of library staff. Work with international library colleagues to organize a conference or training program or focus your state library conference on international issues. Seek opportunities to share best practices and learn from others. Plan to attend the annual conference of the International Federation of Library Associations and Institutions (IFLA) and other international professional meetings and conferences.

Leave home. Join one of the library association's organized delegations to international book fairs where you can purchase books, enjoy cultural events, network with publishers, visit libraries, and learn from colleagues. Join a study tour abroad. Apply for a Fulbright grant or other grants from organizations that support international librarianship. Join an international volunteer organization such as the Peace Corps, United Nations Volunteers, World Library Partnership.

Support libraries overseas by donating funds to purchase materials. Adopt an international library partner of your own or through IFLA or another library association. Become a resource person or correspondent with librarians or library school students abroad.

Increase your global awareness. Learn another language. Take a course in the literature, history, or culture of another country or region. Become a literacy volunteer to teach English as a second language to refugees and immigrants. Read more about the social, economic, political, health, and environmental issues affecting the world. Use your information skills to assist international human rights groups and promote intellectual freedom worldwide.

When traveling internationally, think of yourself as an ambassador for libraries. Contact library associations for material to distribute before you travel, in anticipation of speaking about library programs with colleagues abroad. Offer to write an article about an aspect of international librarianship for library publications, or offer to write about your library association for an international library association publication.

Take advantage of every opportunity to expand your professional global reach and that of the libraries where you work. Today, every library and every librarian can have an international impact and focus.

Embrace Strong Values and Appreciate Differences

Social justice is essential to allowing everyone to develop their full potential through access to strong and vital libraries. Professional values such as access to information for all, intellectual freedom, and advocacy for libraries and users are issues that unite us as librarians around the world. Exposure to professional practices and values in a variety of geographical and type of library settings can lead to thoughtful reflection and stronger values. Values and ethics are at the core of our profession and reviewing and renewing our values in light of changing opportunities and resources is essential for all we do.

Discussing issues with, learning from, and working with individuals from a variety of countries, types of libraries, and backgrounds greatly enrich professional and personal development. The world of librarianship has variety both among our co-workers and even more among those who use our libraries. To make our libraries and our lives all they can be, we must appreciate differences and embrace diversity. Seeking opportunities to expand our exposure to different ideas, people, and work settings can make our careers richer and more fulfilling, and the services we provide our users stronger and more sustainable.

Build Relationships and Collaborative Environments

Empower others by recognizing their strengths, supporting their visions, and encouraging them to think global. Libraries have a key role to play in lifelong and continuous learning for everyone and, as librarians, we must build and sustain relationships that facilitate libraries playing this key role. Respect for the people you work with and serve is essential for all effective programs and projects. People are the basis of all we do and are what makes programs sustainable and effective. Our work shapes and influences every aspect of our life. Open collaborative environments where people can share ideas and learn from one another lead to better ideas and stronger organizations. Our achievements are a sum of many individual decisions and the way to move forward effectively and continuously is to take steps each day. Bold actions will move us forward. Whatever your role in a library, you can contribute to a good working environment with respect and openness to everyone.

Attitude is important in doing what we want to do. Enthusiastic, optimistic people accomplish more and enjoy the journey as well as the destination. Positive thinking leads to hope and inspiration in creating a better world. Libraries are empowering organizations, and enthusiasm and optimism help us fulfill our main functions. Time and energy are among our most valuable resources, and we must share them. To most fully enjoy our life, we must work to resolve all conflicts and develop an understanding of different ideas and approaches to issues. By speaking truthfully and constructively, we can work effectively with a wide range of people. Librarianship is a compassionate profession empowering people to develop and grow throughout their lives. Working in a collaborative environment should enrich our work and our lives and bring us pleasure and fulfillment each and every day.

Collaboration is essential in everything we do. Collective actions and voices are stronger and strengthen the messages we want to convey and activities we implement. We can learn from one another and develop our capabilities to shape our collective destinies. By engaging other people and cultures in collaborative projects, librarians can better serve their users and make better use of resources.

Welcome Change, Remember the Past, Plan for the Future

We must be ready to learn throughout the various stages of our lives. We need to recognize that knowledge changes and grows. A climate of mutual respect and shared responsibilities that exists in most libraries provides a strong foundation for continuous learning. As our libraries have different resources and our users varying needs and expectations, there are opportunities to serve our communities in new and innovative ways. Libraries can be change agents in their communities and lead the community in becoming a better place.

Each of us builds on the activities of those who went before us. The past is a source of enrichment and inspiration as we learn about the efforts of earlier librarians to advocate for their libraries and build strong collections and services in response to community needs. As we build on the activities of those who went before us, we must plan for the future and those who come after us. We must dream of what might be as we create possibilities for our communities and libraries. Positive images of the future allow us to create the world in which we want to live. Imagination is a key to building a better future and vision, leadership and planning will take our libraries into a strong future.

Practice Visionary Passionate Leadership and Advocacy

As visionary passionate leaders, we can encourage and develop creativity and inspiration. Regardless of our positions in library organizations, we are constantly planning for and building our future and the future of the organizations in which we work. Leaders must share a vision of what the organization is, how it will function, and what it can become. Leadership is an attitude cultivated over time, and the goal of leaders is to clearly communicate their vision and purpose. Strong visionary leaders are needed, as libraries look for future opportunities to service their publics. A passionate sense of the potential helps one see the possible. The questions we ask set the stage for what we find out and how we conceive and construct the future. Close emotional ties to the communities that libraries serve build a strong sense of loyalty that is a key to sustaining and promoting libraries.

Becoming a strong advocate for what we care about and believe in is essential in all our work. Librarians in many countries have successfully advocated for increased support of libraries and worked with stakeholders and other interested groups to strengthen access to information for users in many settings. Getting involved in professional organizations on local, national and international levels can add greatly to your professional satisfaction and accomplishments. Advocacy is the responsibility of all library workers and supporters, and professional associations and colleagues can be helpful as we enhance our skills to become strong vocal advocates.

As I have worked with librarians from around the world, I have been very impressed with what can be accomplished with passion, vision and strong advocacy. Library programs and activities must be sustainable to grow and prosper. Programs that build on achievements, existing strengths and local skills best help communities move forward. It is important to keep an eye on how what you plan and do today will be sustained in the future. With visionary passionate leaders and advocates, libraries will continue to extend, support, and sustain a global community.

Act Local and Global

Individuals and groups, taking action on the local level, can change the world. Information has the power to build bridges and promote understanding among diverse cultures. Libraries provide access to worldwide information resources and local accessibility and are central to making the world a better place for everyone. I have been amazed, throughout my career, to see what committed visionary librarians with few resources and little support can accomplish. I have observed this in countries around the world and know that acting locally unites us and enhances our accomplishments. Through local action and global awareness, librarians can continue to expand the global reach and local touch of libraries. Strong local action can lead to the global change we want to see in the world.

Library Values in a Changing World

MICHAEL GORMAN

THIS ESSAY IS ABOUT VALUES, specifically the values that underlie our work in libraries. Some of you may know that the American Library Association (ALA) has had a devil of a time trying to formulate a statement of the core values of the profession. It has consumed the time of two task forces over almost a decade, and the latest product of the second has just been accepted by the ALA Council, largely on the grounds that it consists of a ten-item list without explanation and that list is drawn from various existing ALA documents. This is a stony and contentious vineyard indeed. I am convinced that this difficulty in formulating a statement of values is not only in the usual problems of committees coming up with anything that is snappy and laden with meaning and arguments about wording. These are bad enough, though quite understandable. Think, for example, that a poem is the ultimate example of writing that is snappy, laden with meaning, and all about wording, and then go on to reflect on the fact that there are very few poems written collaboratively and none written by a committee. The central difficulty lies in the fact that the very idea of a value is hard to grasp and easily confused with other beneficial and beneficent things. Just one example will suffice to make this point. The second ALA task force has included "diversity" on its list of core values. Hard to argue with that, one would think, until you reflect on the meaning of the word. In the modern library world, *diversity* means equal representation of all classes of people in a workforce and equal representation of all opinions and cultures in our collections. In other words, diversity is a manifestation of our ideals, desirable because of our beliefs in equal access, equal opportunity, intellectual freedom, etc. The idea of distinguishing between values and desirable outcomes transcends semantics and what many of my ALA colleagues call, revoltingly, "wordsmithing," and goes to the heart of the discussion.

You only have to think of phrases such as "family values" (used extensively by shyster politicians for shady purposes) to realize what a problem the word *values* is. In such cases, the usage is cosmetic. It means "the things I purport to believe in and that you should be made to conform to." We are asked to accept such beliefs on faith and custom, not on the basis of rational analysis. The plain fact is that values *are* beliefs, albeit beliefs that are shared by members of a group, may or may not be based on faith (otherwise known as lack of verifiable evidence), and have been held for a period of time. Given that definition, the next question we have to answer is: Is there a cluster of such beliefs (otherwise known as a value system) that is shared by all librarians? This is a knotty enough question if it is confined to the librarians of today, and it becomes even knottier when we reach into the past and try to discern a golden thread that links us to Callimachus, the great library of Alexandria; the monks of medieval England and their chained libraries; the librarians of the Enlightenment; the great reformist public librarians of the nineteenth century; the long and diverse history of libraries in the twentieth century; and the changing face of libraries today.

Perhaps there is another question we should ask first: Why bother? Since discussion of values can and does revolve around hair-splitting and dispute, why not leave it up to every librarian to sort out her or his own beliefs and destiny? I think there are a number of reasons why any group should seek to create a statement of its values and why librarianship, in particular, should attempt to do so now. The first is the crisis of confidence that we see in some areas of our profession— that existential dread that perhaps libraries will not survive or will be so transformed by digital technology as to be unrecognizable. This lack of confidence leads to the acceptance of the idea that there is no such thing as librarianship— there is no golden thread that links special, public, academic, and school librarians today and librarians of the past. If that were true, then obviously there could be no set of library "core values." On the other hand, if we can formulate and define our values, we can state what we as a profession believe in and what is the essential basis of all library work. The second reason for formulating a set of values is to provide each librarian and each library with yardsticks with which we and they can judge their services and plans. The third reason is that values provide a basis for discussion and some basic premises that we need if we are to work fruitfully with others who work in our libraries. The fourth and last reason is that explicit values are important psychologically to individuals and groups. If individuals and groups share values and act on them, then even failure is bearable, because those individuals and groups know that what was tried was honorable and the effort itself was worthwhile. We live and work in a time in which many librarians are insecure about their work and the future of libraries. Belief in a strong statement of values can be a great thing in dealing with existential anxiety!

In the course of writing my book *Our Enduring Values* (ALA, 2000), I listed eight values derived from previous writings on librarianship and would now like to say some words about them and how they apply to library work today.

Stewardship

There are only three ways in which human beings learn. They learn from experience, and have been doing so for as long as there have been human beings; they learn from interaction with people who know more than they, and have been doing so since the first wise woman passed on the oral traditions of her long ago band of early humans; and lastly, they learn from interacting with the human record, that vast assemblage of writings, images, sounds, and symbolic representation documenting the knowledge of the ages. Humans have been learning in that way since writing and drawing were invented and the age of miracles began. Librarians and archivists (two schismatic parts of the same endeavor) have a unique role in preserving and transmitting that human record on behalf of future generations. I do not use the word *unique* lightly. Many of our values and missions are shared with other groups and interests, but we alone are dedicated to the preservation of recorded knowledge and information. If a substantial amount of the human record were to be available in, and *only* in, digital form, we would be facing a crisis in the preservation of the human record that will dwarf anything that we have seen hitherto. It is imperative that librarians and archivists work together to produce a grand plan for future stewardship that contains practical and cost-effective means of ensuring that future generations know what we know. We should also be stewards of our profession, reinvigorating the library education system to ensure the onward transmission of the values and practices of librarianship.

Service

Librarianship is a profession defined by service. We serve both individuals and humanity as a whole in what we do. Every aspect of librarianship, every action that we take as librarians, can and should be measured in terms of service. Our service can be as large as a successful integration of library instruction with undergraduate curriculum or as small as a single brief act of helpfulness to a catalog user—but it can and should pervade our professional lives so that it becomes the yardstick by which we measure all our plans and projects and the means by which we assess success or failure of all our programs.

Intellectual Freedom

Intellectual freedom can be defined quite simply. Individuals are entitled to think and believe whatever they wish, and that freedom to think and believe is vitiated if access to words and images conveying the thoughts and beliefs of others is restricted. Allowing others to have access to writings and images of which you approve is easy; the difficult part is allowing equal access to writings and images of which you disapprove. The book banners, film burners, and record smashers are always with us. People who do not believe that you should be allowed to read and see things of which they disapprove are found in every society. The classic reasons for that denial are sedition, blasphemy, and obscenity, and though the latter has been the focus of censors for the last few decades ("To the impure, all things are impure"—Oscar Wilde), sedition is making a comeback in Bush II's America (see the obnoxious USA Patriot Act) and blasphemy cannot be far behind given the tide of socio-religious fundamentalism on which Bush II surfs. Librarians believe in intellectual freedom because it is as natural to us, and as necessary to us, as the air that we breathe. Censorship is anathema to us because it inhibits our role in life—to make the recorded knowledge and information of humankind freely available to everyone, regardless of faith or lack of it, ethnicity, gender, age, or any other of the categories that divide us one from the other. I strongly believe we should be absolutists when it comes to intellectual freedom and carry out our tasks without reference to our own opinions or the opinions of those who want to restrict free access to knowledge. I should acknowledge that, as an academic librarian, I am comparatively better off than fellow librarians in other areas. We work in institutions that are overwhelmingly dedicated to the idea of academic freedom; we tend to work for people who share that ethic; and we are usually not professionally isolated. Compare that context to the lonely battles that are fought by American librarians in small, rural public libraries and by solitary school librarians battling obscurantist school boards. If you look at the lists of challenged and banned books that are issued each year by the American Library Association, you will see that those are the people on the front lines. All the more reason to support our library associations' offices of intellectual freedom in the great work they do on our behalf to protect this most important professional value.

Equity of Access

Intellectual freedom in libraries is inextricably linked to equity of access. Much is made of the "digital divide"—the idea that the poor and other disadvantaged have less access to technology than others. I believe the digital divide is a part, and not the most significant part, of a societal divide in the United States, and one of the features of the societal divide is the library divide. It is too often taken for granted that if you live in the United States and are poor, handicapped, a member of a minority, very young, very old, and/or live in a rural area, you will not have access to the full range of library services, just as it is taken for granted that your access to health care, education, and other goods of a civilized society are similarly trammeled. It is important to beat the censors and make all library services accessible to everybody without fear or favor, but it is equally important to ensure that such access is practically possible and not biased in favor of the better off or the more powerful. Such unfettered access is brought into question by some aspects of technology and by the tide of privatization. The idea of charging for access to library materials and library services is much more popular today than it was before and the whole virtual library idea is, essentially, an elitist construct that writes off sections of society as doomed to be information poor. I am not saying that libraries that use technology intensively as an enhancement to their services are inevitably going to betray the value of equity of access, but I am saying that there are some inherent contradictions in society and in our use of technology that should make us very sensitive to the idea of maintaining libraries that are freely available to all—irrespective of social standing and economic circumstances. The ideal library of the future will be one in which access to all materials and services (including electronic materials and services) will be freely available, without barriers imposed by lack of money or lack of technological sophistication. This value is especially important to those academic libraries like mine that serve a population containing a majority of economically disadvantaged students.

Privacy

A major affliction of American public life today is the wholesale and largely successful attack on the right to privacy. Letters are read, traps are laid, e-mails are reconstructed, bookstore records are happy hunting grounds for inquisitors, the most private aspects of lives are laid bare to be condemned and sniggered over, and the right to your own thoughts, your own relationships, and your own beliefs is trampled on by zealots and bigots. This is the world of 1984, the world of mind control, the world of mental totalitarianism. The confidentiality of library records is not the most sensational weapon in the fight for privacy, but it is important, both on practical and moral grounds. In practical terms, a lot of the relationship between a library and its patrons is based on trust, and in a free society, a library user should be secure in trusting us not to reveal what is being read and by whom. On moral grounds, we must start with the premise that everyone is entitled to freedom of access, freedom to read texts and view images, and freedom of thought and expression. None of those freedoms can survive in an atmosphere in which library use is monitored and individual use patterns are made known to anyone without permission.

Literacy and Learning

Libraries are an essential part of the culture of learning because of the importance of our contribution to making the human record accessible. The flight from books and reading that can be seen in the writings of the more fervid technophiles among us is a flat betrayal of the history and culture of libraries. The importance of the interaction between the scholar or student and the text transcends the medium used to convey that text. An illiterate with a computer is, essentially, no better off than an illiterate with a book. Literacy is much misunderstood today; it is not a simple question of being able or unable to read. True literacy is a process by which, once able to read, an individual becomes more and more literate throughout life; more and more able to interact with complex texts and, thereby, to acquire knowledge and understanding. It is a key element in the enterprise—learning—to which all libraries are dedicated. Instead of seeing the world as divided between the illiterate, a-literate, and literate, we should see literacy as an open-ended range of possibilities in which librarians, educators, and students work together to learn and become more learned using sustained reading of texts as a central part of the life of the mind. In this respect, the distinctions between kinds of librarians become unimportant—a children's librarian or school librarian is as important to the early stages of literacy and learning as a public librarian or academic librarian is to the later stages. We are all involved in the same process: providing the materials, instruction, and assistance that enable individuals and societies to grow and to thrive intellectually.

Rationalism

I am sure that I am not alone in being distressed by the great tide of fundamentalism, superstition, and plain craziness in the world today. From religious bigots to faith healers to militants of all stripes, the world seems to be full of people who are convinced that they know the One True Way and are aggressively intolerant of those who do not share their beliefs and prejudices. I think that our profession is, above all, a child of the Enlightenment and of rationalism. Libraries stand, above all, for the notion that human beings are improved by the acquisition of knowledge and information and that no bar should be placed in their way. We stand for the individual human being pursuing whichever avenues of enquiry she or he wishes. We also stand for rationalism as the basis for all of our policies and procedures in libraries. Librarianship is a supremely rational profession and should resist the forces of irrationalism both external and internal.

Democracy

Democracy, in name if not always fully in practice, is now the dominant global political idea. It is an idea that depends on knowledge and education. It is a sad irony that as American democracy has reached its theoretical ideal—the enfranchisement of all adults, irrespective of gender and race—it is in danger because of an increasingly ill-informed, easily manipulated, and apathetic electorate. The rights for which revolutionaries, women, and ethnic minorities fought are being vitiated by a culture of sound bites, political ignorance, and unreasoning dislike of government. Libraries are part of the solution to this modern ill. As an integral part of the educational process and as a repository of the records of humankind, the library stands for the means to achieve a better democracy. The best antidote to being conned by TV is a well-reasoned book, article, or other text. All our other values and ideas are democratic values and ideas—intellectual freedom, the common good, service to all, the transmission of the human record to future generations, free access to knowledge and information, non-discrimination, etc. A librarian who is not a (small d) democrat is an almost unthinkable idea. Libraries have grown and flourished in the soil of democracy and our fate is inextricably intertwined with the fate of democracy.

Not only is the environment we need to succeed one of democracy, but we should commit ourselves to democracy within the library. I am as heartily sick as the next person of the annual management fad to which American universities seem to be fleetingly addicted. What is striking about all the alphabet soup of management fads (MBO, TQM, etc.), apart from their barbarous management-speak and their essential similarity each to the other, is the fact that they all embody values and ideas that have been commonplace in many libraries for decades. It is always galling when it dawns on one that the name of this year's management fad may be different but, essentially, it is preaching the same old cooperation, tolerance, participation, mutual respect, encouragement of innovation and diversity, etc. They always add up to what a former colleague of mine called "applied feminism" and are manifestations of the democratic nature of well run libraries.

The General Good

ALA's second task force on core values included the phrase *the public good* in their list of values. I did not include it or any synonymous term in my list of values, but I do believe it goes to the heart of our discussion of all these matters. Social conservatives in the United States are fond of talking about *culture wars*—a term that posits a divide between those who have a paternalistic, militarist, repressive, and reactionary view of the world and those who do not. If you worship the flag, are antifeminist, deny the value of public service (other than the kind in which people get killed), and believe in censoring books and artwork, you are in one army, and if you are a feminist, pro-civil rights and equal treatment under the law, and believe in intellectual freedom, you are in the other. Even worse, if you are a pacifist and tired of wars on this and that, and the metaphorical use of war images, you are beyond the pale. To my mind there is a conflict that is wider than these cultural and societal hot button matters. It is the gulf in thinking and social policy that exists between those who believe in individualism and those who believe in the greater good. The late great Mike Royko said that the motto of the city of Chicago should be *Ubi est meum?* ("Where is mine?") I would suggest that that attitude is not restricted to that great city and that a tax-phobic, selfish, government-hating tendency is a major force in American society (and not, from my reading, an entirely unknown force in Canada). Such people do not believe in the greater good—that impulse that sees investment in social institutions as good because societies are improved when its citizens are healthy, educated, and literate. Perhaps, when it comes down to it, *this* is the overarching belief that underlies all our values—a belief that is selfless, optimistic, idealistic, and progressive and that reconciles the rights of the individual with the greater good of society—and provides the answer to the question "Why are libraries important?" That answer being "Because libraries and librarians contribute to all that we value about society—the greater good."

Note

This essay—an edited version of a keynote speech at the Canadian Library Association annual meeting in June 2004—is based on, and in some cases quotes verbatim, my book *Our Enduring Values* (ALA, 2000) and a number of other writings and speeches in the last few years.

Librarianship: Intersecting Perspectives from the Academy and from the Field

KEN HAYCOCK

A s I prepare for this essay and reflect upon my thirty-five years as a professional librarian, I am struck by the proverbial sense of "déjà vu all over again."

The issues facing the profession appear to me to remain pretty much the same, although the context may vary. The principles and perspectives are largely the same, although the tools and techniques may have changed. Our notion of forward motion is, regrettably, illusionary. Although I find this lack of progress somewhat depressing I also cannot help but be eternally optimistic when our potential continues to be undiminished. Let me explain.

Have libraries changed in the past four decades? Certainly our technologies and systems are more sophisticated than ever before and allow for greater access to resources and independence of use. But what we do remains fundamentally the same—and that is good. We still focus on a specified community of users (whether geographic or organizational), collect resources (both physical and virtual data objects) for that particular community and its needs, organize this information for ease of access and knowledge production, preserve the human record (although archivists would argue about our use of that phrase), provide programs and services to improve connections to information and ideas for that unique community, and ensure quality management such that the orchestration of players and funds results in valuable and valued services delivered effectively and efficiently for the maximum good.

What then remains purposeful and constant?

Librarians work in a variety of environments, some of which are libraries.
This statement is deceptively simple and self-evident yet it is at the heart of

the debate over "library education". For years I could not pinpoint my differing and discomforted point of view with many of my educator colleagues until I realized that many educators believe that we are educating "information specialists" many of whom may work in libraries, while I believe firmly that we are educating professional librarians, many of whom may choose to work other than in libraries.

While director of an ALA-accredited graduate program in Library and Information Studies (among others), I welcomed our new students each year and encouraged them to think about librarianship as a profession and vocation and not simply about libraries as institution and place. I encouraged them to believe that they would make exceptional historical researchers, information analysts, journalists, staff developers and Internet trainers and these were legitimate and important roles for librarians. I remain concerned about the shift from librarianship to a homogenized "information studies" that threatens to move us from our core values centered on the user's needs and the public's right to know.

Our values are constant yet we seem unable to express them.

When academics and practitioners came together for the first Congress on Professional Education one note of discord (among many) was heard around core values. As Chair, I positioned the clarification and articulation of our values as the first of more than forty recommendations for bridging the gap between the academy and the field and improving education. After all, if the profession wanted graduate education to ensure the continuation of attention to core values it needed only to specify them and embed them in standards for accreditation. We provided a timeline of six months but three years and two task forces later, the profession is still unable to fashion a succinct statement of values. What other profession, so immersed in value-laden propositions about service, could remain so divided and inarticulate? Each new statement focused more on orientations, civic obligations and ethics than on values unique to our profession. Wordsmithing became a blood sport among the survivors of the language wars of the 1960s and no consensus was reached about values as debate took place on the veneer of language and interpretations of words.

Are we not committed to informed decision-making as a foundation for democracy through service for all, access for all, freedom of expression and inquiry for all, privacy for all, and maintenance of the records of the human experience? Of course it is more complex and deeper than this but a profession unable to lift the plough and agree on some lofty principles and values is not complex, merely bifurcated.

We continue to lack confidence in our abilities and uniqueness.

There are too many academic and public libraries that do not engage library technicians as they "cannot" do the work of a professional librarian. Too often a staff member in close proximity to a shelf cannot answer a simple question without referring the customer to the reference desk. Too often a trained technician cannot provide simple reference service in the evening (why should professionals work the hours we are open?) but an untrained graduate student can. It seems that we would rather provide poor service than competent service if the replacement might suggest capability similar to a librarian. Surely we can demonstrate competence through performance rather than drawing lines in the sand. The end result is that technicians are replacing public, school and special librarians and subject specialists replacing librarians in academic libraries. If we concentrated on performance and articulating our uniqueness rather than rising up in defensiveness we would be better appreciated and supported.

Libraries try to play too many roles.

Libraries can certainly be all things to all people, with adequate funding. But who has unlimited funds? It appears that we wish to emulate the Hard Rock Café's mission: *Love All; Serve All, Save the Planet.* I would argue that the most successful libraries, regardless of type, have clearly defined role statements that reflect both their users' needs and the research into impact on its community's development. The "community" in this context might be a law firm, a school, a university or a municipality. Librarians appear loathe to define roles and priorities, however, because somehow it is exclusionary—our message is that we would rather do too much, poorly.

Research into school librarianship, for example, indicates clearly that teacher-librarians who focus on student learning place a high priority on collaboration with teaching colleagues and have a higher impact on student achievement; teacher-librarians who also provide formal and informal staff development opportunities for colleagues enjoy higher administrative and financial support.

And what has changed, and in my opinion, for the better?

There is no longer a "public good", only demonstrated "public value".

The age of entitlement (show me the money) is over. The age of accountability (here's is what we do and why and how well) is here. Misty-eyed academics do their students a grave disservice in not making this abundantly clear and providing the strategies to be effective in this new environment.

When I was an elected school board president and later city councilor I was struck by the number of residents who questioned expenditures on "public goods" like schools and hospitals and libraries. I came to learn that these public institutions could still be well-supported, if they demonstrated high return on investment. Yes, ROI, a business term.

There has been a fundamental attitude shift from supporting public services as a "good" thing to supporting public services because they enhance the quality of life in their communities in demonstrable ways. In other words, a school library can demonstrate a specific contribution to the improvement of student achievement, a public library can demonstrate an improvement to business development, an academic library can demonstrate how it has contributed to the enhancement of scholarship, a special library can demonstrate how it has saved monies or improved profits.

This paradigm shift has been accomplished by a shift in evaluative criteria by which funders judge their libraries. Inputs (dollars per capita) are seen less as a measure of support than as a measure of efficiency (less could be better). Outputs (circulation, reference transactions) are seen more and more as largely meaningless (and believing that decision-makers *should* value them is a zero-zero game). The prevailing focus is on outcomes, not the number of books circulated per capita but the calculated impact on literacy, not the number of new databases for business but how those resources, combined with a specific service focus, improved the efficacy of home-based businesses in the community.

Librarians need to get with the program and demonstrate value. This is not difficult but it creates dissonance in our prevailing culture. We prefer to be "shocked and appalled" by the behaviors of decision makers and funders (a.k.a. the great unwashed).

Our business is a business.

We say that "it is not about us" but about the customer (patron if you insist). We despair about being a service not a business. (Of course the world's largest business, Wal-Mart, would argue that it too is a service.) One board on which I served used to joke that for librarians the "F" word was finance—and this was a board of librarians. Every time a dollar changes hands there has been a business transaction. We establish a mission based on our values, we plan strategically and allocate resources accordingly, we engage competent and capable staff to make our products and services available, we monitor and adjust depending on our market's needs and desires. These are all business activities. In my executive search business for public library directors one of the first questions we get from boards and city councils is "do we really need a librarian or would we be better off with a CEO?" We start by examining how they need not be mutually exclusive. However, more and more "chief librarians" in academic and public libraries (as well as school and special actually) are not librarians and this trend will only continue if we do not develop the requisite skills in management and leadership.

Our business is community development.

How often have you heard the story that the problem with the railroads is that they thought that they were in the railroad business and if they had only realized that they were in the transportation business they would have approached their work much differently and not only survived, but thrived. Speakers at library conferences then proceed to explain that librarians can no longer think of themselves in the library business but need to become competitive in the information business if they are to survive. My experience suggests that this is wrong-headedness.

While it is true that libraries can no longer stand alone as silos dedicated to the public good, they need to recognize that they are in the community development business. A municipal library needs to demonstrate how it improves the quality of life in its community; a school library needs to demonstrate how it contributed to the development of a community of learners.

This means that we need to become much more astute at expressing ourselves in the language of the community, connecting agendas for win-win propositions, respecting as equals the community's leaders and decision-makers and recognizing that the community's criteria for evaluating library success may be much different from ours (I have yet to meet a city councilor who thought that reference transactions was a meaningful indicator of anything—especially when we can't even say how many were answered accurately and to what effect).

The client may not be the customer.

Without engaging in the debate over whether we serve patrons, users, customers or clients (although I confess to a preference for customer as service improves with a customer orientation, or client as our customers do indeed pay for a professional service even if "only" through taxes), the focus of librarians is changing. Children's librarians, for example, have long provided an exceptional professional service for young people who use the library for education and recreation; however, there is at least an emerging debate over whether the primary client should be the children themselves or their caregivers. Consider the implications of program objectives. Is the objective of youth services to enhance family literacy?. Is family literacy in a community improved more by high quality direct service to young people in the library or through the training and support of day care supervisors, preschool workers and primary teachers in children's literature and its exploitation through skilled storytelling, story reading, puppetry, and book talks? Of course it is not an either/or proposition but with limited resources librarians are starting to examine greatest impact for return on investment in ways that have not occurred before.

Similarly, law librarians are examining support for communities of practice within the firm rather than single lawyers. They are looking at product- or service-based charge back to lawyers rather than time-based billing to demonstrate bottom-line savings for repeat searches and research products. College librarians recognize that course-integrated instruction has to start back with the assignment and integrating the librarian into the process as a faculty equal before direct service to students will be effective. Working with intermediaries and direct "supervisors", whether faculty or parents, librarians may provide the customer with better service and support overall.

And what has not changed and remains deeply problematic?

Library culture is inherently unhealthy.

For the longest time I couldn't understand the norms of behavior in many libraries. I thought that colleagues simply lacked self-confidence and interest in a career ladder. Then I took an MBA and started to do more management consulting work. I learned to apply labels to cultural norms. My initial observations were tested on other management consultants, trained outside our discipline but who worked in libraries on management issues such as strategic planning and organizational development. Let's keep in mind here that there are great libraries with positive cultures—focused on problem-solving with an eye on continual improvement. But there are many more that reflect two overarching norms: the debilitating sense of victimization and complete conflict avoidance.

Librarians and library workers have made a professional pastime of complaining about salaries, working conditions, lack of appreciation. The irony of course is that libraries are run by librarians and there are innumerable examples of efforts to improve beginning salaries only to be flummoxed by negotiating teams refusing to focus on the neediest among us.

I began my professional career as a teacher (and teacher-librarian) where the code of ethics was clear and specific: you badmouth a colleague to a supervisor or another colleague, without informing the person first, and you could lose your right to practice, and there were many examples of this happening. In librarianship, it is a professional pastime to badmouth colleagues behind their backs. It is interesting that of my graduate degrees only in my MBA program was a unit on ethics required (some readers are no doubt thinking that the reason is obvious, but that is not my experience). Our code of ethics focuses only on the user, not our behavior toward each other. We prefer to smile in meetings and despair in the halls and washrooms. It seems to me that people who are unwilling to place the organization's problems on the table for discussion and debate like adults have no right to complain outside the decision-making rooms and offices where meetings are held. Victimization and conflict avoidance make minor library problems major stumbling blocks to improvement.

So why would one be optimistic?

We understand better today our unique role and impact.

Although we need more research into our profession and its impact I would offer some emerging propositions.

Librarians have a unique contribution to make to their community, however defined. Librarians are knowledgeable navigators who connect people with information and ideas. We are learning to reposition ourselves as expert community developers who connect with the agenda of community leaders and opinion leaders. We improve community assets. We operate from a unique neutral public space that allows us greater opportunities for partnerships and fund development. We can demonstrate return on investment as a public value.

Librarians differ from other library workers. Of course we have professional preparation and graduate education. Beyond that, however, my interviews with librarians who have also been technicians, and employers of both, suggest that librarians differ in three ways from library technicians. First, we understand deeply the principles and theories undergirding our expertise and roles; we are thus able to move easily from position to position within the organization. Second, we manage people and resources within the organization, and market to meet client needs (marketing being different from advertising and public relations, instead focusing on client needs and desires and adjusting systems to meet those needs); indeed, this management/marketing role seems to enhance status and salary. Third, we develop and train staff and users, staff to deliver the service (we are often the only professional in a branch) and users to undertake more simple tasks themselves (librarians in a newspaper library train journalists and staff to do simple searches themselves). Regrettably, most of our education programs prepare us well only for the first of these three roles.

Librarians have enormous scope for career choice. I could never quite understand how one became a "former" librarian. It seems to me that once you are a librarian you are a professional for life, regardless of you career title. When I was a school principal and senior education official I was occasionally introduced as a former librarian. I always then began my presentation with an explanation of how grateful I was in my current position to have the experience and skills of research, of organizing information, of having an organization-wide perspective, of making decisions based on evidence rather than opinion, of managing people and resources based on values; indeed, I felt that many in senior administration were impaired by not having this particular education and experience.

More of our graduates should enter other fields on graduation; more of our graduates should move through the organization, out of the school and special library, and into the hierarchy of the organization—this never means one stops being a librarian or even stops practising one's profession.

We have credible models for success.

Medical librarians save lives—we know this from our research. School librarians have a positive impact on student achievement—we know this from our research. Public librarians change lives—we know this from our research. We have both individual and organizational models of success in communities across the continent. We need to make known these success stories and see them as our own. Too often we treat success among colleagues with the Australian "tall poppy syndrome"—by cutting them down for the good of the crop. We need to recognize that when each of us succeeds, we all succeed.

We have hope in our new professionals.

For more than ten years now I have been a mentor for the Northern Exposure to Leadership institute, held every eighteen months for emerging leaders with two to seven years of professional experience. Each time someone asks me why I would volunteer a week of my time to participate. The answer is quite simple. There can be no greater joy or hope for the future than to spend a week with younger leaders who can articulate their role in society and demonstrate the skills to realize their and their organization's potential. Further, they are committed to continual learning and continued improvement for themselves and their organizations.

My work suggests that we need more graduates who choose librarianship as their first professional career choice (an unexpected finding from three different studies), who recognize critical attributes for success, including leadership ability and skills, who can demonstrate, or learn to demonstrate, extraverted behaviors and who welcome connections with community leaders and civic agendas.

This is a wonderful discipline and a wonderful profession. It never ceases to amaze me that so many opportunities can present themselves, that corporate and geographic mobility can be so easy, that there can be so much room for so many exceptional individuals. Of course, one has to prepare, one has to participate, one has to make connections, but these are relatively easy in a service profession popu- lated with transformational leaders.

Librarianship is unique. Let's not lose it in an ill-defined "information stud- ies" morass.

Meet the New Boss, Same as the Old Boss: A Personal View of Librarianship

PATRICK JONES

O
NCE UPON A TIME, I managed a department that provided library services to teenagers in the correctional system. When training a new librarian to provide this service, she asked an innocent question about serving these young men and women found guilty of crimes. The question was simple, strong, and sobering: "why?" That is, why did we provide this service, and what did we hope to achieve in terms of outcomes for the prisoners and outputs for the library? My response was this: "Good question. I don't know."

The organizationally correct answer would have been to haul out high-level verbiage from the library's vast inventory of visions, missions, overarching goals, and strategic directions all created with good intentions. All these documents loaded with the usual suspects of buzzwords that said everything, and in doing so, really said nothing. But even then, that wasn't the real question. The real question was why I personally thought this work was important, and why I thought this work mattered to these young people, and I guess, to myself.

When working with youth in libraries, we have the ace in the hole by playing the "children are our future" card, which like lots of clichés, and library vision statements, sounds good on paper, but doesn't hold up. For these kids in corrections, as well as the ones in our libraries using computers or even checking out a book, they couldn't care less about the future; so what can we do for them today? To fall back on the "tomorrow's taxpayer" line of thinking is the same: it views young people in libraries simply as a means, not an end. Moreover, the "tomorrow's taxpayer" argument isn't really about serving young people; it is about self-serving our own institutional drives. It's a public library; thus, the people's needs come first, and our wants second. Thus, I chant the Clintonion mantra: "It's about the public, stupid."

Yet, so often, especially in working with teens, we discount what that public wants from us because we know better than they do. At the height of the *Goosebumps / Fear Street* craze, so many youth librarians were still wringing hands trying not to get them dirty by allowing such "trash" in their library. In doing so, they created something more horrifying than R.L. Stine could have imagined: libraries that told kids what they wanted didn't matter. That was then, this is now, so let's look at graphic novels. I'm not a comic book reader, so I have no personal stake in this issue, but I'm professionally offended by the same ugly arguments dusted off to deny teens' access to graphic novels and comic books. It is much easier now than in the budget rich nineties to blame shrinking collection dollars rather than the real issue: we just don't get it.

Libraries often view services to teens, including collecting graphic formats, as "special" and outside of their normal mission. Example: most public libraries collect large print books. They collect them primarily to meet the needs of one customer segment, seniors. Seniors read large print because changes in their bodies cause eyesight to fail and thus the library responds with the large print format. Example: most public libraries collect board books. They collect them primarily to meet the needs of two market segments, toddlers and babies. Toddlers and babies need board books because changes in their bodies cause them to want to hold books but they are without the developmental skills to not want to rip them up, and thus the library responds with the board book format. Example: some public libraries collect comic books and other graphic formats to meet the needs of teenagers, but many don't. Collecting comic books and graphic novels, and other popular materials, is not about doing anything special for teens, just doing the same as we do for other members of the public. It's about the public.

But who is this public and what is this library? Look at the twenty-first century challenges we face: new technology, patrons not just new to libraries but new to speaking English, not enough staff or resources or space or political support, and the normal litany of library laments. However, as the great poet Pete Townsend told us: "meet the new boss, same as the old boss."[1] This situation is not unfamiliar to American public libraries; it is ingrained in our roots. So, let's look at those roots and get back to the question at hand: what are we doing here on the most basic level. For me, libraries are about making connections between people and information, which the public not the public librarian defines. This is what we have always done and will always do. At one point, we chained the books to the shelves where now we unchain every possible information need through unlimited Internet access.

Access is so easy in theory; so hard to practice. For most of us, this isn't really what we do every day, is it? No, instead, we put paper in printers, sign up people for computers, and then kick people out for using too much paper or looking at "inappropriate material" on those same computers. We spend more time rounding up Accelerated Reader (AR) titles than rounding out kids with access to great books that failed the test of having an AR exam written about them. Is this why any of us entered this profession? Many days we all must question our career choices.

Recently, I rediscovered why the library matters by not looking inside the profession, but outside of it. In doing so, I could see my work in the larger context of what it did to create community, not just ten hash marks on the tally sheet. I recovered my passion for public libraries at the Search Institute (www.search-institute.org) through their "forty developmental assets" framework. The forty development assets are the factors critical to a young person's successful growth and development. These forty assets are positive experiences, opportunities, and personal qualities that all youth need in order to be come responsible, successful, and caring.

The key research finding is this: the more assets young people have, the more likely they are to thrive as teens, then become caring competent adults that contribute to society rather than taking from it. No, the assets are not the holy grail of solving every youth problem, but the strength based asset approach is research grounded, easy to understand and sell, and all the evidence suggests this: it works. Despite all of the changes anyone who has worked in libraries for over twenty years has seen, this model tells me my work still matters.

Back-story: I was not a library user growing up in Flint, Michigan. I recall, and often retell when training library staff members on serving teens, having a negative experience when I did use a library in middle school. Going to the public library to find books for a school report, I ventured to ask if the library also carried magazines concerning my number one interest: professional wrestling. But no, the library did not have any wrestling magazines, and for that matter, the tone of the librarian's response suggested there was something wrong with me for assuming the sacred stacks of this citadel of lifelong learning would be littered with magazines about grown men in their underwear pretending to hurt each other. Thus, I left the library thinking, as the walking nerve that is the middle grade mindset, that there was something wrong with me for liking wrestling, rather than knowing this librarian had failed to purchase a ticket on the clue train. I left vowing never to return to this and any other public library. I'd buy my wrestling magazines, get my stuff for school reports at school or at home in the encyclopedia, and that's what I did, until I went to work in a library in my senior year in high school. Because I loved books, reading, and lifelong learning? Not at all. I took the job as a library page because it was easy work, and I didn't have to wear a uniform or cut my hair. As I advanced in my career, I sadly learned all three of those initial assumptions were wrong.

I was fortunate enough in that entry level library experience (shelving books) to work for someone who soon let me go beyond just putting books away and doing small things like working the circ desk, calling reserves, etc. So, when a para-professional job came up, I applied and got it. The day I started in the job (which varied from twenty to forty hours a week), I was told that I started in the union and I was earning a pension. Thus, if I stayed on, went to library school, and came back, I could retire at age 47. This had very high appeal to me. But beyond that, I found out during those early years that I really liked library work: I liked customer service, I liked collections, and I liked helping people make connections. I also found that I was pretty good at it, so that certainly swayed my decision.

Finally, like most folks, as college was winding down, I was thinking about how I was going to earn a living. My hometown of Flint in those days had unemployment well into the double digits (the more things change . . .) and jobs for English/Political Science double majors were rare. Thus, I went right to library school and had my first professional job by age twenty-three. Well, twenty years later, I don't think I will be retiring at forty-seven and the landscape of libraries has certainly changed, but I find that the things I liked back then are the same things that keep me wired to this profession providing the public with access to lifelong learning, defined very broadly.

But how does playing a computer game or reading a wrestling magazine contribute to lifelong learning? That's not learning, that is playing. Wrong. The young adults doing these things in a school or public library are learning something else, something more important: the value of libraries. They should be learning that libraries are an important part of any school and in every community. Strong communities tend to have strong schools and libraries. We'll never be in a position to build assets if we don't get them into the tent. We won't be positive role models by chasing kids out of libraries who are engaged in a perfectly legitimate use of resources. Within the boundaries of community based policies and anti-porn statutes, the public chooses its own acceptable use. Repeat with me: it's about the public.

We know this. We know that young people with assets are more likely to contribute to, rather than take from, society. We know the cost to the community in social services, corrections, and other institutions of kids without assets. We know that libraries can and do build assets. Thus, libraries build communities. Assets create positive outcomes and positive outcomes create stronger communities. We serve teens because libraries build community.

Connecting young adults and libraries is not about treating teens "special," but it is about serving them uniquely. Just like services to other market segments of the public library: toddlers, genealogy, seniors, college students, and small-business people. Each group of users has different demands upon libraries due to different needs based on what it is trying to accomplish. Above all else, teens are trying to accomplish one thing: forming an identity. If we believe that libraries are good things for a community, then does it not follow that we want teens, as they are forming this identity, to recognize this value? If we believe libraries have value, then we will want teens to learn that by our deeds and action. If we believe that our work has value, then we need to know that it matters. If we believe that libraries should be supported by the community, then we need to show and prove to the community that libraries matter. Communities allocate resources based on what they value.

We have moved from inputs, to outputs and now to outcomes. The stimuli are varied, but an over-riding motive is to "prove" our value so our public will continue to fund libraries. We have tried to prove that for years with outputs: here is how many people are using our library; here is how many books were checked out, etc. Three problems, of course, emerge from clinging to this as our primary approach. Continuing to invest in circulation as a measure is buying a commodity that is sure to decline as we move more information resources into electronic format, trying to keep up with teens' mad rush thinking they can just ask Jeeves. We are no longer the only game in town; funders and even our beloved public are wondering why we need school and public libraries—just give kids the Internet. Finally, given competing demands, our public wants to see what effect we really have; they are wondering if we make kids lives better? Demanding to know what is the value in an after school program? A summer reading program? We are better at counting numbers of books checked out than lives changed.

We measure circulation of young adults books, but what really matters most is the outcomes we create in young adult lives. The question is no longer only asking what does a young adult find in a school or public library when they enter it, but also asking what happens to that young adult as a result of checking out a book, attending a book discussion program, spending time as a student assistant, or learning how to locate information on the Internet. Librarians serving teens don't just develop collections; they help in the vital process of developing young people to become competent, caring adults. Libraries do not, should not, and cannot develop services for young adults because it is good for the library, but rather because these services will make an affirmative impact leading to positive outcomes for teens. Libraries are in the youth development business working to develop positive assets in the lives of teenagers.

Wrong, you say, I'm not in the youth development business. I want to come to work, do my teddy bear story time (complete with crafts!), order beautiful picture books, and go home. Well, going home is a good idea because it's not about the cute finger play, the glue sticks and construction paper, and its not about picture books that librarians love that bore kids to tears. Just like it's not about pointing "over there" at the reference desk: Pop quiz: what's it about?

I've managed to avoid addiction to most computer games, except one: Sim-City, where the object of the game isn't to kill things, but to build a community that works. Maybe it's a product of growing up in Flint, but the appeal of game, that you can take a broken community and fix it, or a build a new one from the ground up, is pretty damn appealing. Yes, I still need to build jails in my Sim cities, but the more libraries you build, the higher the education level and the lower the crime rate. One great way to increase the education of your citizens is to build libraries, one in every community. Like I said, it's just a game, but the intent is real.

Now, I think I'm ready to answer that question, "Why?" Why provide library service to teens in corrections, or any teens, or any member of the public? Because it fulfills a larger social good to create the sadly maligned phrase of an inspiring vision: because it creates a great society. But nothing is that simple: does it create a great society to provide young African American men (strike one) convicted of a serious crime before the age of eighteen (strike two) with reading materials celebrating rap artists whose vision is often not of a great society, but of a hedonistic, homophobic, women's role as hos, and the heavenly place of pimpin'? Is that strike three? How can you say "we build community; we build assets" on one hand, while on the other actively providing access to reading materials that say, more or less, to hell with everyone else, it's about what I want. It's not about a great society, but who's got the most gold rings?

Yes, for some of these young men, re-enforcing these arguably negative role models is not keeping with the asset model. For some, not all—not even the majority. We all say repeatedly that reading is powerful enough to change lives, only taking credit for positive change, but somehow sneaking out the backdoor at the very idea that somehow reading could be harmful. We'll tell our boards proudly about the teens that got better grades because of our work, but we'll fail to mention the kid who checked out *Mein Kampf* from the library and is now serving time for curbing the non-Aryans among us. As the grand proto-punk band Gang of Four told us: "we all have good intentions, but all with strings attached."[2] We should advocate for access but be aware that many teens, as well as other members of our public, won't use this access to engage in lifelong learning or build internal and external assets.

What do we hope to achieve by working in libraries with young people? It comes back to assets and access: we want to provide young people with access to information (in the broadest sense) so they can thrive, build assets, and become caring competent adults, who realize it's not all about them. Sometimes assets and access conflict, and we use our best judgments and best intentions to massage the conflict, achieve compromise and build community. We do this work because we're trying to have a society, and while our work sometimes has blowback, it is mostly about providing a foundation where every person can walk in our door (real or virtual) and have a positive experience. Do libraries change lives? No, because libraries are full of breaking down computers, poorly displayed books, and bad carpet; it is librarians who change lives. Librarians like you and, I hope, me. Meet the new boss: same as the old boss, so don't get fooled again thinking your work doesn't matter.

Notes

1. The Who, "Won't Get Fooled Again," *Who's Next*, Decca Records, 1971.
2. Gang of Four, "Damaged Goods," *Entertainment!* Elektra Records, 1983.

The Fog of My Career: Some Reflections and Lessons Learned (with apologies to Errol Morris and Robert S. McNamara)

GILLIAN MCCOMBS

> *"Through the act of writing you call, like the ancient* chamana, *the scattered pieces of your soul back to your body. You commence the arduous task of rebuilding yourself, composing a story that more accurately expresses your new identity. . . . [W]riting is an archetypal journey home to the self,* un proceso de crear puentes *(bridges) to the next phase, next place, next culture, next reality."*

—GLORIA E. ANZALDUA

ALTHOUGH I HAD JOTTED DOWN scraps of notes in the months since asked to write this essay, and even made a list of points I thought would be useful, it was not until I watched the documentary *The Fog of War: Eleven Lessons from the Life of Robert S. McNamara,* that a format and theme crystallized in my head. Joseph Lelyveld of *The New York Times* once said that when we talk about Vietnam, we are seldom talking about the country, or the people and their situation. Usually we are talking about ourselves and probably always were. In case you are wondering if you haven't opened the wrong book, or if I haven't written the wrong essay, the moral of this tale is that everything is personal—your career, your life, your lessons learned. The deeper part of this moral is that it is impossible to separate out the professional from the personal. I am who I am. I have made the choices I have made because of who I am. And by extension, the lens through which I look back on my career and ahead to the future of the profession is also exquisitely personal.

Lessons Learned

Context is crucial for understanding my 'lens.' I was born and educated in England, a country with a strong tradition of the scholar librarian. When I was eight or nine years old, I played libraries, not dolls, and took great pleasure in glueing book pockets and charge cards into my personal library, fining my younger sister for scribbling in my books. I had been 'the librarian' in grammar school—a position of enormous power, giving me the ability to deny my class-mates borrowing privileges if they lost or failed to return books. I had always known I was going to be a librarian. The only refinement of this goal was the realization, one sunny day in Latin V while studying for my university entrance exams, that I would become a University Librarian, not work in a public library (in spite of the fact that my grandfather had been Chief Librarian of the local public library, and had carved his initials in the large wooden bowls used to col-lect the fines, before he departed to establish a traveling theater company before the First World War.) **Lesson No. I: Everything is personal.**

Library school followed university, and oh, what a let down! How to make the transition from discussing neo-platonism, Marsilio Ficino and Marguerite de Navarre to discussing the merits of local government funding for public libraries and the Dewey Decimal versus Library of Congress classification systems? A like-minded friend and I survived the eternal tedium of library school by doing *The Times* crossword puzzle on the back row of class and arguing violently about inconsistencies in classification schedule interpretation. Needless to say, my marks were dismal, although I was recognized for my classroom debating style and gen-eral 'bolshy' character. Credit was not given for contribution in class. This was a library school before OCLC, before the MARC record, before any kind of auto-mation except punch cards, which were beyond my power to comprehend. A field trip to the National Lending Library for Science & Technology in Boston Spa, designed to show us the way of the future in document delivery and interlibrary loan, turned me off field trips for ever.

The Library Association (the British equivalent of the American Library Association, now known as the Chartered Institute of Library and Information Professionals) functioned much more as an old fashioned craftsman's guild or trade association than a professional society. It administered the credentialing exam, and several years of on-the-job experience were required before being allowed to affix the letters A.L.A. (Associate of the Library Association) after one's name. In 1968, I interviewed for a position at Hull University Library but was turned down by the consummate scholar librarian (and poet and jazz critic), Philip Larkin. I had no philosophy of librarianship, I did not want to bring literacy to the poor or information to the disenfranchised. I just wanted to bury myself in the books, the quiet and the familiar, avoid talking to anyone, and reflect my way through life. **Lesson No. 2: A philosophy of librarianship takes time to grow; one is not born with it.**

That is not to say we library school students in the late 1960s didn't look for meaning in our lives and futures—we did. There were bus trips to London to participate in sit-ins outside the American Embassy to protest the Vietnam War but at that time in my life I could not see a reason to be involved. Life on the home front was pretty dreary. Our library school dean was in a walking coma— his wife had been killed in a car accident the summer before I arrived and he never recovered. Our classes were mostly filled with people already working in public libraries who thought we university graduates were snobs. My friend and I tried to reconcile our dreams of the cloistered book lover's life with the dawning realization that our chosen profession could turn out to be a deadly bore.

My first professional position was head of the music library at Huddersfield Public Library, West Yorkshire, although I had interviewed for the position of assistant librarian at the Technical College. In those days, interviews for a library position in local government consisted of bringing all the candidates together one afternoon and having each one of them meet sequentially with the library board. At the end of the afternoon, the successful candidate was announced and everyone else got to go home and get on with the business of looking for a job. It seemed in this case that the library board, in its infinite wisdom, managed to see past my carefully 'spun' resume that highlighted every single minute I had spent in biology/science classes to the evident truth that I was much more suited to the position of music librarian at the public library. **Lesson No. 3: Never underestimate the abilities of other people to better see what you should be doing than you yourself.**

A requirement of my job as head of the music library was participation in the musical life of the community. But what did that mean? Was I expected to play in a quartet or sing in a choir? No, luckily for me, it turned out that all I had to do was attend concerts—in particular the annual Christmas ritual of Handel's *Messiah*, sung by the Royal Huddersfield Choral Society whose members used my library regularly. **Lesson No. 4: Never be afraid of what the job seems to entail.** It is often both less and more than you envision. An interview will never test you on the things you think it should, but always send you curve balls that will test your potential for fitting into the institution's culture.

The main focus of my job was to select materials for the music library— books, scores and recordings—and act as circulation/reference librarian. The highlight of my day was to put a big sign on my desk—"Librarian in Soundproof

Room"—and close myself off in my listening room to 'test' the new releases. I was unfamiliar with the concept of 'collection development'—one just bought the best that was out there with the money one had—but did feel I needed to add a few contemporary composers for variety and so as not to show favoritism.

A less pleasing part of my day was when patrons would actually come by to check out the recordings. They had to present them to me to be checked against a map on the sleeve that recorded any scratches. When returned, the records had to be re-examined for additional damage. It was one of the toughest moments of my career when I had to inform one of my favorite patrons—an elderly near-sighted gentleman—that he would have to pay for the record due to a huge new scratch, in spite of his protestations to the contrary. I was so traumatized by the incident that I avoided him for the duration. The most dread-laden part of my job, however, was my monthly Saturday morning stint at the main circulation desk. The lines were long, the people were loud and the trays of oblong cards impossible to keep in order or retrieve under pressure. The date stamps were blurred, the cards never there. The people were grouchy and impatient, often wet and soggy from the elements outside. Too many books had been chewed by dogs or had pages ripped out by babies. I was a disaster at the circulation desk and could not wait for the opportunity to run for cover to the music library. **Lesson No. 5: Know thyself.** Learn your strengths and weaknesses and, as you proceed along your chosen path, hire people who can provide the strengths or skills you lack. I was clearly not suited to a job in public services.

Newly married, I arrived in the United States in 1970 and focused on settling into my new country. By the time I left for Vietnam in 1973 with my journalist husband and two little girls, I was desperate for intellectual stimulation and adult discourse. I looked for work at the British Council library in Saigon, not realizing that employment of the host country's nationals was part of its philosophy. I tried the American Women's Association, but that library was well supplied with volunteers to dole out the numerous mystery and detective paperbacks that counted for most of its shelf stock. After the Fall of Saigon in 1975, I found myself back in Washington, D.C., still jobless, almost husbandless, and with friends who asked 'where were you the last couple of years?' **Lesson No. 6: Sometimes life is hell and you just have to get through it.**

While waiting to hear from the various academic libraries I had applied to, and not understanding that a glacial response rate was the norm, Lady Luck decided to nod her head in my direction. The friend with whom I was staying had a friend who was a librarian at Dumbarton Oaks—one of Harvard University's many outpost research facilities. There was a vacancy in the Garden and Landscape Architecture Library. **Lesson No. 7: Never underestimate the role of** external events or 'Lady Luck' to shape your destiny (often known as your 'career'); and **Lesson No. 8: Establish a multidimensional network of friends and contacts, personal and professional.** It is often 'who you know' that can tip the balance in any one direction.

Although I went through library school in the B.A. and B.O. years (Before Automation and Before OCLC), in 1978 I supervised one of the first implementations of OCLC at Dumbarton Oaks. This was my first 'conversion' although I did not then know enough to call it such. Like most other libraries at that time, we ordered LC card packets and filed endlessly. It took me many years to figure out just what OCLC did apart from spewing out catalog cards. The concept of 'bibliographic utility' did not resonate at that time in my blinkered, uninformed, uncontextualized life, when working in a library was the only thing I knew how to do to support my two (about to become three) daughters, when single parenthood seemed to be a given in my future, when looking for a job so I could survive on my own with my girls was all I thought about—not my career or 'advancing in my profession.'

In 1982, I needed to make more money. **Lesson No. 9: Fear can be a great motivator.** It was intended that I become the sole provider for our family in order for my husband to write his Great American Vietnam War novel. Being even a partial stay-at-home mom was not an option. What was I to do? **See Lesson No. 7.** Lady Luck again nodded her head in my direction. I happened upon a copy of *Library Journal* carelessly tossed onto a shelf in the Department of the Interior library where I was cataloging books on contract. Flipping through the pages—I had never even heard of the journal, such was my cluelessness—I found two positions advertised at the University at Albany, SUNY—a cataloger and Head of the Catalog and Shelflist Maintenance (CASM) unit. Not understanding the job description for the latter, I applied for the position of cataloger. The Albany personnel officer called to say that although I was obviously well qualified for the cataloger position, the search committee thought I was better qualified for the position of Head of CASM. Could I be persuaded to apply for that position instead? I agreed reluctantly, thinking that they would certainly change their minds once they met me. I had no way of knowing that my experience (which by now included selling real estate to make ends meet, acting as general contractor on the renovation of a four story brownstone, supervising a slew of contractors and managing six rental properties) was the kind of background the library was looking for in order to restore morale and bring order out of chaos to the unit. It had become known as 'the CASM' in no small part because of what happened, or didn't happen, to books that went there.

I came back from the interview convinced that I could never work in such a political, unhealthy, manic/depressive place—and in a basement to boot! **Lesson No. 10: Never say never.** I stayed at Albany for 16 years in that windowless basement. I moved from Head of CASM to Assistant Director for Technical Services and Systems, made many long-lasting friendships, raised my three girls with a lot of help from the CASM staff and my colleagues, earned my MPA and met my beloved husband-to-be. Yes, gentle reader, I married him—the Dean of the Library School! Isn't that corny? And yet, what wonderful arguments we have had bandying back and forth the relative merits of theory and practice, and working together to lobby for lifelong learning and libraries. **Lesson No. 11: Never lose your excitement and passion for what you are about, and always go for those big, hairy, audacious goals!**

We met while both of us were trying to save a collection of 5,000 historical children's books—wonderful runs of the old series books such as *Nancy Drew, The Hardy Boys*, the *Five Little Peppers* and *The Motor Boys*. The collection was sitting on the radiators in the old graduate library at Albany, literally disintegrating. The inferior wood pulp paper was not designed to last a lifetime, just for a few enthusiastic readings or so. Albany's leading criminologists were infuriated by seeing those books (disparagingly known as 'kiddie lit') shelved near their legal treatises. Our crusade was successful, however, and the books were speedily removed from those radiators to safekeeping in CASM. The collection was eventually named after its chief benefactor, Miriam Snow Mathes, has more than doubled in size and is housed in its own endowed special collections room.

Throughout the fog of one's career, there will be, if one is lucky, some galvanizing moments when the heavens and stars align themselves with earth and there is, for a brief shining moment, a lightening bolt of true clarity. I have been blessed by several such moments: for instance, walking into a promotion and tenure meeting and opening my mail—reading the letter from the New York State Council on the Arts (NYSCA) awarding me and a colleague the first grant funding for the children's collection. Another such moment came several years later in 1993. Sitting at my desk and reading the article in the *Chronicle of Higher Education* about a techie in a Swiss laboratory and a software application called Mosaic—the first 'killer app'—I knew instantly that this would revolutionize the profession and persuaded a colleague in network services to download it immediately on my PC. **Lesson No. 12: Trust your instincts and go with them!**

Sometimes you might be wrong. (I was wrong about the NYSCA grant. It took a lot more persuading and campaigning to save that collection.) But more often than not, you will be right. You will also probably be ahead of your colleagues and co-workers. That is what true leadership requires—skating to where you hope the puck will be, not to where it is, to mangle the over-used Wayne

Gretzky quote. You should be thinking ahead to what that next killer app might be—whether it is a technical product, a revolutionary service, or an unmined cache of primary resource material. It will take all your leadership skills to bring the rest of the world along with you. But without a vision, without a sense of where you are going, you will do little more than get through the day.

How did I get to Dallas, Southern Methodist University and a deanship? **See Lesson No. 3.** I had certainly gone as far as I could at Albany with promotion to full librarian. I was not really in the market for a Ph.D., although the School of Public Administration was anxious to sign me up. Teaching at the library school was something I had flirted with, but see **Lesson No. 5.** I was a pretty hopeless teacher. I could handle the odd guest lecture and the semesterly visitation to my department from the Information Processing (former Cataloging & Classification) Class, but that was all. Now that my girls were all grown and the last one in college, I began to think I might relax a little on the job stability front and take a few risks. Having completed my MPA in 1995 and learned a lot more about organizational culture, management, leadership, budgets, economics and even labor laws, I felt better equipped to be at the top. In spite of my inner lack of confidence and insecurity, the rest of the world seemed to think I was ambitious, extroverted and extremely self-confident (read opinionated and still 'bolshy' although America uses different adjectives!) Perhaps it was time to start living up to that reputation.

Perusal of the *Chronicle of Higher Education* ads became a regular part of my week, with the pluses and minuses of each directorship debated hotly at the kitchen table. There were several tentative forays into the job market. Again, **Lesson No. 3** prevailed. In spite of my conviction that I would be perfectly suited for a small college library, no small college library seconded my opinion. I needed to think a little bigger. At last there was an ad in the *Chronicle* that seemingly had my name on it. The university in question desired a library director who was technically savvy but still set high store by books and traditional resources. The only problem, it was in Dallas, Texas—home to John Wayne and J.R. Ewing—and a far cry from our small upstate New York town. However, remember **Lesson No. 10? Never say never!** I applied and from the first round of interviews it seemed like a match made in heaven. The people were wonderful, they loved their libraries, and they seemed to love me. The rest is history!

Conclusion

One never stops learning. The lessons I have clumsily attempted to convey to the reader are just the most obvious ones learned as I muddled through the fog of my career. There are many other lessons that I have learned over the years—about management, leadership, organizational culture and people—but those must be saved for another article. Robert McNamara proposes his lessons in the hope that they may "advance peace among nations in the twenty-first century." I do not presume to think that my 'lessons learned' will bring about any such glorious gain. However, my years in Texas have taught me the value of listening to people's stories. They give humanity, depth and color to our lives. What could be more important than hearing stories from another time to help explain our roots and how we got to where we are today?

The fog of our career will often swirl around us and blind us to the fuller sense of what is happening. Think of Fabrizio del Dongo in Stendhal's *La Chartreuse de Parme*, looking for the battlefield, not realizing that the Battle of Waterloo was actually going on around him. So are we in the fog of our lives where nothing is clear except in retrospect. We bear witness and tell our stories. It is up to you, the reader—the profession's future—to gain strength from our collected histories, from our lessons learned and our mistakes made, from our successes and our failures. As Cicero said, "Not knowing what happened before you were born means being a child for ever. For what is human life, unless it is interwoven with the life of our ancestors, by the memory of ancient history." I hope my story will enable you to find transformation in your life or perhaps the validation you need in order to keep on going with your chosen path. Remember **Lesson No. I: Everything is personal.**

> Do I dare
> Disturb the universe?
> In a minute there is time
> For decisions and revisions which a minute will reverse.
>
> *The Lovesong of J. Alfred Prufrock*
> T.S. Eliot

Note

The Fog of War: Eleven Lessons from the Life of Robert S. McNamara, Sony Pictures Classics presents @radical.media & SenArt Films production in association with the Globe Department Store; producers, Michael Williams, Julie Ahlberg; produced & directed by Errol Morris. Edition: Widescreen (1:78:1) anamorphic. Published: Culver City, Calif.: Columbia TriStar Home Entertainment, c2004.

References

Anzaldua, Gloria E. "Beyond Traditional Notions of Identity." *Chronicle of Higher Education* 49, no. 7 (11 October 2002). Adapted from *This Bridge We Call Home: Radical Visions for Transformation*, ed. Gloria E. Anzaldua and Analouise Keating. New York: Routledge, 2002.

Cicero. *Orator*. 46 B.C.

Eliot, T.S. *The Lovesong of J. Alfred Prufrock*. 1915.

McNamara, Robert S. *Argument Without End: In Search of Answers to the Vietnam Tragedy*. New York: Public Affairs, 1999.

Suggested Readings

Brand, Stewart. *The Clock of the Long Now: Time and Responsibility*. New York: Basic Books, 1999.

Harvard Business Review

Kekes, John. *The Examined Life*. Lewisburg: Bucknell University Press, 1988.

Rybczynski, Witold. *A Clearing in the Distance: Frederick Law Olmsted and America in the Nineteenth Century*. New York: Scribner, 1999.

Anything by Peter Drucker

Everything by Edward Tufte

Social Justice as a Context for a Career in Librarianship

KATHLEEN DE LA PEÑA MCCOOK

REFLECTING UPON MY CAREER and what has been important and will be important to librarianship has been a difficult task. To accomplish this, I have summarized my career trying to identify key events that influenced me, tried to describe the convergence of ideas, and listed books that I am currently using.

Out of the Streets, into the Palmer House, and Back on the Barricades: Twentieth Century

My mother, Margarita de la Peña, a defense factory worker from New Mexico met and married my father, Frank Eugene McEntee, a radioman with the U.S. Navy, during World War II in Los Angeles. Neither one had finished high school. They moved to the Chicago area after the war and we lived in several trailer parks until settling in York Center where I went to high school at Willowbrook. Unusual for those days, York Center was a community cooperative and comprised of people from all ethnicities. I was fortunate to grow up this way.

Although York Center was unincorporated and had no library, my father used a friend's address to get us a card to the Elmhurst Public Library. This was in the 1950s, just a few years after publication of *A National Plan for Public Library Service* (ALA, 1946). Lowell Martin's chapter, "The Potential Role of the American Public Library" noted: "An adequate purposeful library should be brought into the life of every American" (p. 17). How true this was for me, but the LSA had not yet passed, and a false address was needed. My father was a union electrician (Dupage IBEW Local #701) and told me that he could probably help any future husband get into the union. When he left union work we counted, I guess, among the working poor. I had a work permit at thirteen.

I graduated from the University of Illinois at Chicago Circle in 1969. Public education was the key to my entire career. My tuition was $400 a year, and I really did waitress my way through. During my college years I was a member of the Young Socialist Alliance; protested the War in Vietnam; volunteered on the West Side of Chicago in April 1968 when Rev. Dr. Martin Luther King Jr. was assassinated; campaigned in Milwaukee for Eugene McCarthy; marched in the protests at the 1968 Democratic convention; and substitute taught in Pilsen, the city's largest Latino community at that time. I graduated with a degree in English and went on to Marquette University on a fellowship for a master's degree in the same. At Marquette I protested after the Kent State shooting, and my time there was heavily influenced by the Catholic Worker movement. One of the other students was married to a librarian. I met Philip Heim there, whom I later married. His mother was a school librarian. My future was clear. I taught eighth grade math in Kankakee, Illinois, to save up for library school and attended the Graduate Library School (GLS) at the University of Chicago in 1971–1972. Paul Wolfowitz was there at the same time, but we never met. The *Bulletin of the Atomic Scientists* was published in Hyde Park. I remember that they moved the Doomsday Clock back during the SALT talks in 1972. Guess they didn't know about Paul.

Another big event for me in 1972 during my GLS studies was accompanying a group of students and Professor Lester Asheim to the Palmer House hotel to meet Robert Wedgeworth, the new Executive Director of the American Library Association (ALA). I didn't know then that the Palmer House hotel would be my second home in the late 1970s and 1980s as it was often headquarters for both the ALA and the Illinois Library Association conferences. I also got married in 1972 and accepted a position as reference librarian at Rosary College (now Dominican University) in River Forest, Illinois. Most of the themes that have shaped my teaching, writing, and professional service—human rights, equal rights and civil rights, social justice, support for labor, and peace—were laid out by experiences growing up and in college:

When I entered librarianship Michael Harrington's *Other America* (1962) and the report "Access to Public Libraries" (ALA, LAD, 1963) had been analyzed and discussed broadly in the field. Eric Moon of *Library Journal* wrote of the *Access Study*, "It has opened many doors of inquiry . . . for example the suggestion that patterns of discrimination in employment of minority group members in libraries should be studied is an excellent and tenable objective" (*Library Journal*, Feb. 15, 1964, 817). To respond to these concerns ALA established the Office for Library Service to the Disadvantaged in 1970, now the Office for Literacy and Outreach

Services, to promote the provision of library service to the urban and rural poor, of all ages, and to those people who are discriminated against because they belong to minority groups; and to encourage the development of user-oriented informational and educational library services to meet the needs of the urban and rural poor, ethnic minorities, the underemployed, school dropouts, the semiliterate and illiterate, and those isolated by cultural differences; and to insure that librarians and others have information and access to technical assistance and continuing education opportunities to assist them in developing effective outreach programs.

The very existence of OLSD/OLOS as a focal point of ethical concern within ALA coupled with the Social Responsibilities Round Table (SRRT) provided me with a strong rationale to become an active member of ALA. I've tried to document ALA's journey to achieve "Equity of Access" to all people in several publications including the essay "Poverty, Democracy, and Public Libraries" in *Libraries and Democracy: The Cornerstones of Liberty* (ALA, 2001) and the report "Rocks in the Whirlpool: The American Library Association and Equity of Access" (ALA, 2002). I chaired the OLOS advisory committee during its twenty-fifth anniversary and worked closely with then director Mattye Louise Nelson to honor the first director of OLOS, Jean E. Coleman in 1996 at the New York annual conference.

I was a librarian at Rosary/Dominican during the Illinois Minorities Manpower Project, a specially funded project for recruiting minorities into librarianship, I worked there on World Hunger inspired by Sister Alice O'Rourke and Peoria's Bishop O'Rourke of whom Dorothy Day wrote in 1971, "He's the Rural Life Bishop and loves Chavez." I volunteered at the Public Art Workshop organizing clipping files about Paul Robeson and Diego Rivera and helped with a mural protesting the CIA's involvement in the assassination of Chile's Marxist leader, Salvador Allende. The women's movement was a special focus and I attended consciousness raising groups. Library systems were new and I was able to help with a test among LIBRAS colleges to install the first OCLC terminal for Rosary. Library cooperation in the greater Chicago area in the early 1970s was rampant, contagious, and fun. Barbara Ford, then a documents librarian at Illinois, would give me her discards for our less well-funded collection. I attended meetings of the Illinois Regional Library Council, Suburban Library System, and Illinois Library Association.

Because Rosary/Dominican had a school of library science the idea of teaching came to me, and I was encouraged by Linda Crowe, Dominican's most engaged faculty member who introduced me to Kathleen Weibel who welcomed me as a colleague and lifelong friend at the University of Wisconsin–Madison's Ph.D. program. I commuted via Greyhound bus from Chicago to Madison, Wisconsin, my first year and worked with Kathleen and members of Wisconsin Women Library Workers on the SRRT Feminist Task Force bibliography of women in librarianship, which became *The Role of Women in Librarianship* (Oryx Press, 1979). My daughter, Margaret Marie, was born in 1978. My dissertation under the supervision of Jim Krikelas was on data archives and assessed ways to study social inequality. At Wisconsin the work of two adult services scholars, Helen Lyman and Margaret E. Monroe, imbued me with an understanding that literacy and adult education had to be integrated with library access issues.

Hired to teach at the University of Illinois Graduate School of Library and Information Science in Urbana–Champaign I taught government documents and library administration and worked very hard on the ALA and ILA Equal Rights Amendment Task Forces. When Peggy Sullivan was ALA President she appointed me to Chair the ALA Committee on the Status of Women in Librarianship and I worked with the legendary Margaret Myers of the Office for Library Personnel Resources (OLPR) on a variety of projects aimed at pay equity between men and women, expanding the pool of new librarians by recruiting more intently among people of diverse ethnicities, and documenting the careers of women of color. The ERA did not pass but the work of the chapter of Illinois Women Library Workers with Katherine Phenix, Martha Childers, Julia Hansen, and others dedicated to the cause of equality burned bright. My favorite photo of my daughter, Margaret, is of her at two, marching with librarians at the Chicago Mother's Day March organized by NOW in 1980.

Recruited to be the Dean of School of Library and Information Science at Louisiana State University in 1983, I devoted myself to the kinds of mid-career challenges you'd expect: working with amazing students who have become the leaders of today; getting my school into the top ranks; working with a grant from the Council on Library Resources; conducting research; being active in professional organizations including president of ALISE. The Adult Services in the Eighties Project was carried out for the Reference and Adult Services Division of ALA that involved a collaborative team of researchers including Bert and Judy Boyce, Gary Rolstad, Connie Van Fleet, Danny P. Wallace, Bill Moen, with great support from Library Science bibliographer Alma Dawson (now a professor). It has been one of my career's high points that the book we did together, *Adult Services: An Enduring Focus for Public Libraries* (ALA, 1990), is still broadly cited. I made dear friends. I got divorced. I edited *RQ* and *Public Libraries*. I was chair of the ALA Office for Library Personnel Resources advisory committee and did studies of occupational entry and the need to recruit among diverse populations. I was appointed dean of the graduate school. I remarried to Bill McCook.

In 1993 I was recruited to the University of South Florida School of Library and Information Science in Tampa where I was director for six years. Long a member of REFORMA, I felt that working in an area with a larger Latino population might give me an opportunity to work harder in extending services to Latinos. The school won a federal grant to hold an Institute on Library Services to Seasonal and Migrant Farmworkers in 1998 and sponsored the Trejo Foster Institute on Hispanic Library Education in 1999 (*Library Services to Youth of Hispanic Heritage*, McFarland, 2000). It was a highpoint in my tenure to work with Arnulfo and Ninfa Trejo on this event. I stepped away from administration in 1999 and was appointed Distinguished University Professor, a post I hold today free from management duties. In 2002 I was honored with the Trejo Award for REFORMA Latino Librarian of the Year. I am an active member of my union, the United Faculty of Florida, and serve on the collective bargaining team.

The election of Jeb Bush as governor in Florida (who would try to close the state library in 2003), the theft of the presidential election in 2000 (with the Florida debacle), the move from an academic model to a business model at the university, and the dismantling of the statewide faculty union combined to startle me into action. Since 2000 my whole focus has been to conceptualize how libraries might serve the ideals of human rights; equal rights and civil rights; social justice; labor and peace. I have consciously sought writing and speaking opportunities and association activities that will allow me to examine and write about these issues. My husband Bill, a union carpenter, and I have protested the war in Iraq at the gates of McDill AFB, where CENTCOM is located. We have worked on grass roots campaigns to regain democracy to the exclusion of all other activity. From the 1968 demonstrations in the streets against the War in Vietnam, a long tour of duty in the Palmer House and administrative suites in the 1970s, 1980s, and 1990s, I entered the new millennium back on the barricades.

Social Justice and Equity: Toward a Librarianship That Fosters Human Capabilities, the 21st Century

At the outset of the twenty-first century I made a sincere effort to consolidate major themes I had been thinking about since 1968 into a series of essays and articles. My book on the role of libraries and community building, *A Place at the Table*, was published as a project of ALA's first millennium president, Sarah Long (1999–2000) and my study of libraries and their commitment to the poor was included among books of essays on libraries and democracy edited by the second, Nancy Kranich (2000–2001). After librarianship's utter immersion and infatuation with all things Internet in the 1990s, it seemed to me that a major reconnection was needed with the idea of the library as a vital community center. In addition to the book, I launched a website and mailing list, "A Librarian at Every Table," which counts over 800 subscribers and has archives of 250 editions (*www.cas.usf.edu/lis/a-librarian-at-every-table/*).

The "Campaign for America's Librarians" initiated by ALA President Mitch Freedman (2002–2003) focused on work and labor issues for librarians and was emblematic of the national exodus of worker's rights. Underemployment, failure to raise the minimum wage, and massive tax cuts for the top income earners are aspects of a larger class warfare perpetrated by the greed-driven right wing in control of this nation who wish to destroy public education and diminish access to health care. By providing support to labor and information to those seeking better employment librarians can help achieve social justice.

The tragic events of September 11, 2001, opened the way for the U.S. government under its first appointed president, George W. Bush, to move toward a repressive environment. The swift passage of the USA Patriot Act and its expectation that libraries and bookstores would open their records to government agents caused a split among librarians. This coupled with the effects of filtering and CIPA legislation underscored a censorious undertone that has disappointed me, but also re-enforced my commitment to writing about the need for a free public sphere. To some degree higher education has been at fault, and I thus examined the need for civic engagement among schools that prepare librarians as well as connection to community organizing, adult education, and literacy providers.

In Florida, a number of actions took place that have given me a close-up lesson in the vicious and ruthless political action for the gain of the far right wing. In 2003, Florida's governor, Jeb Bush, sought to close the state library. It is my belief that Bush was being vindictive toward a profession that had sought to provide truth and this was one of what he called "devious plans" to undercut the people's right to education. Bush was angered that librarians had invited a speaker to a conference critical of the way the 2000 presidential election (that ended up with the appointment of his brother) had been handled in Florida. I don't think Bushy anticipated the grass roots effort that librarians would make to beat back his order for closing the library. While the state library remained, Bush was successful in creating some divisiveness within the Florida profession that will not easily heal. The state has a state librarian, appointed by Bush, who supported closing the state library.

Also, some public library meeting room policies were challenged. Local governments fearful of hosting speakers who might be critical of the religious right closed meeting rooms. At the school where I teach, an online discussion list that was discussing the lead-up to the Iraq war in language critical of the government was shut down without notice. Faculty were directed to censor other faculty. As people are less and less likely to post information because of fear of reprisal there will be less information available. A chill is in the air. It is not popular in 2004 to fight against filtering but to allow filters in public libraries or to steer discussion away from the political means a diluted exchange of ideas. Authentic discourse is killed by intimidation. Too many think saying nothing is acceptable. We must resist.

Librarianship in the twenty-first century will recommit to human rights on a massive scale. We will fight the oppressive forces that hold that security trumps freedom. If necessary we will establish truth commissions like *Nunca Mas* that get to the bottom of repression of the public sphere. Science will be respected again, not squelched as it has been since 2000. Librarians will be the ones to ensure that truth is preserved in spite of a government that detests science, use the FCC to stifle dissent, holds secret meetings on issues of national importance like energy policy, and directs its military to stage false events such as the toppling of Saddam's statue to give the appearance of acceptance of occupying forces.

The truth in matters international, political, social, and economic is vital to the growth of human capabilities. Officials such as Florida's Governor Jeb Bush have sought to destroy the spirit of librarians and this destructive intent must be countered. Librarians must bear witness to the violence done to humanity in the name of security by preserving records and making them available. Libraries like the University of California, Santa Cruz with a website of documents on Iraqi prisoner abuse at Abu Ghraib by U.S. forces demonstrate the power of libraries to offer the soil in which truth grows.

Paul Farmer, writing of the pathologies of power, describes the preferential option for the poor espoused in liberation theology and the need to act, especially in matters of health. Librarians, too, will need to reassess philosophies and determine actions to give preferential treatment to poor people and the homeless. Over the last several years I have worked with American Library Association president Carla Hayden (2003–2004) to document the Association's Action Goal of Equity of Access. Until every single person has equal access to the human record, we cannot rest.

Philosophy Begins in Wonder and Ends in Performance

JAMES G. NEAL

OES LIBRARIANSHIP have at its core a philosophy, or better a world view or weltanschauung? Is it evidenced by what we as librarians do, or what we say, or how we are understood and perceived? Has our persistent struggle to define a set of fundamental values and ethical principles shaped this philosophy? Has the growth of the profession in terms of both its size and diversity of roles and settings undermined our ability to articulate and apply a philosophical basis for our work?

Philosophy, in its original and widest sense, means the love, study, and pursuit of the knowledge of things and their causes. This can be both theoretical and practical, or what Aristotle referred to as *contemplative* and *active*. Philosophy has trifurcated into branches or lines of thought, namely, natural philosophy or science, moral philosophy or ethics, and metaphysical philosophy or knowledge. Certainly, librarianship has a basis that rests in knowledge, science, and ethics. More particularly, philosophy connotes a set of opinions, ideas, or principles, or perhaps the system that an individual forms for the conduct of a life. Does a commonly shared philosophy of librarianship underpin or perhaps just influence what a librarian believes and how a librarian behaves?

As Plato writes in *Theaetetus*: "Philosophy begins in wonder." This sense of arousing awe, of surprise, or perhaps even of admiration may explain the attraction of individuals to librarianship. One could argue that the magnetism of librarianship as a profession is rooted in the fundamentals of its work. The focus on a core set of services to users is attractive, and these include: information acquisition, that is, building library collections of relevance and quality; information synthesis, that is, organizing collections for effective access and use; information navigation, that is, seeking and locating needed materials; information dissemination, that is, delivering content where, when and how it is needed; information interpretation, that is, evaluating and harmonizing content to address a particular requirement; information understanding, that is, educating users to become knowledgeable and independent; and information archiving, that is, preserving content for long-term availability.

Layered on top of these perhaps traditional activities is a set of other strategic functions that further exemplify the "wonder" of the field. The opportunity to improve the library as study, research community, cultural, social, and intellectual space and the ability to create virtual counterparts to physical places are attractive professional challenges. The mandate to employ and integrate technology in innovative ways to improve access and services and to promote individual and organizational productivity is shifting the basic infrastructure if not the fundamental knowledge base of the profession. The urgency of developing and organizing and managing human resources stretches professional talents as libraries seek to become less bureaucratic and hierarchical and more collaborative and compassionate. The expectation is that librarians, in particular those in administrative roles, will define success not only in terms of the ability to allocate and expend financial resources to advance organizational goals, but also to build new sources of funding through fundraising, grants, marketing, and entrepreneurial business activities. The leadership role and the visibility of the library in the communities it serves, and the librarians in the professional and political circles to which they are attracted, are increasingly relevant to satisfaction and advancement. But are these "administrative" responsibilities at the core of the professional philosophy? Does librarian as space planner, technologist, manager, fundraiser, and community leader also define what the profession is about or simply add further clutter to the superstructure of the field?

And to add additional burden to the definition of librarian roles and responsibilities, the experience of the past decade has thrust the profession into new arenas that could be argued on the one hand to have shifted the philosophy of the field or, on the other, to have undermined the basic tenets or beliefs. Does the philosophy of a profession drive professional choices, or do fundamental expansions of activity redefine philosophy?

For example, as librarians have become more sophisticated consumers, and as negotiated and licensed access to electronic content has become so dominant, has the profession become more market rather than philosophy driven in its collection building role? As the work of librarians is increasingly linked to complicated layers of collaboration with diverse groups, has the philosophy of librarianship been compromised or perhaps polluted by the values of strategic partners? As libraries take on the functions of publishers and educators, in competition or in cooperation with community, academic and corporate agencies, does the philosophy of profit if even just cost recovery shift the basic outlook of the field? As libraries advance research and development activities and pursue technology transfer objectives in support of professional, organizational, and national priorities, do venture capital and business planning begin to dominate rhetoric and practice? And as librarians become increasingly embroiled in legislative and legal policy activities, do these advocacy roles and the hardball nature of political alignments contribute to compromising of professional philosophy?

But is the philosophy of a profession rooted in its work, or are aspirational statements of basic policies a better guide to core beliefs? The library profession has been very aggressive in formulating, disseminating, and upholding such affirmations. Whether it be the "Library Bill of Rights," the "Code of Ethics," statements of "Freedom to Read" or "Freedom to View," or outlines of foundational values that guide professional practice, librarianship in the United States has long championed the articulation of such policies.

Therefore, as librarians perform their roles in their institutions and communities, the professional judgments made on a daily basis in libraries should be directed by these principles. As Timothy Leary, the controversial U.S. psychologist and Harvard professor, noted in a 1989 London *Evening Standard* interview: "In the information age, you don't teach philosophy . . . you perform it. If Aristotle were alive today, he'd have a talk show." So in many ways, the true test of a philosophy is performance.

Scanning across the policy statements of librarianship, one can identify many principles that librarians struggle to advance individually in their assignments and collectively through the work of professional associations. These statements, in many ways, address Isaiah Berlin's "two concepts of liberty," that is, "freedom to" or positive and assertive actions, and "freedom from" or negative and defensive actions. Many of the principles of librarianship capture the characteristics of both notions. Thus equity of access can mean that all library users should have ready access to information as an assertive right, or it can mean that barriers to access, such as cost, technology, format, or content must be defended against. Similar schizophrenic interpretations apply to the values of confidentiality/privacy, diversity, intellectual freedom, and social responsibility, for example. In addition to these civic concepts, librarianship also advocates certain professional objectives. These include, for example, lifelong learning, professionalism, service, preservation of information, fair use, integrity, affirmative action, literacy, and globalization. Rooted in these concepts is a clear distinction between personal convictions and professional duties, and a basic premise that libraries are a public good and that librarians act in the public interest.

Having ruminated briefly on the convergence of philosophy and librarianship, I should now turn my thinking to a more personal reflection on the philosophical roots and development of my own sense of the profession. There are several key events, or perhaps better, realizations that explain my thoughts, and these, I would argue, are common among those who "back into" librarianship as a vocation. I was very late to the understanding that, in fact, librarianship is a career, with its own professional roots and conventions, its own professional status and mandate. I was initially amazed and baffled that there is a field of professional study culminating in a graduate degree that qualifies one to work as a librarian. The link between librarian and library did not seem as obvious as the connection between doctor and medicine or between lawyer and the law, for example. A subsequent awareness of the diversity of the places and assignments where the talents of librarianship could be invested and developed was an important transition in my appreciation of the possibilities. It confirmed, in my case, that an individual committed to a life in the university, focused on research and writing, interested in administrative advancement, wanting to influence the political process in the public interest, and needing to be engaged in the world could find a challenging and lifelong home in librarianship. Thus, I bring an academic library bias and an administrative disposition to my thinking about the philosophy of librarianship.

For over thirty years, I have pursued these professional and personal aspirations costumed as an academic librarian. This has certainly been a revolutionary period in the life of the profession. I often state something like the following in my presentations on the future academic library: Fundamental changes in higher education, information technology and scholarly communication are provoking a radical revisioning of the future academic library. The library must pursue strategic thinking and action, fiscal agility, and creative approaches to the development of collections and services and to the expansion of markets. Higher education libraries are advancing away from the traditional or industrial-age library, a model that is no longer viable. The combined impact of digital and network technologies, the globalization of education and scholarship, and the increased competition for resources will produce a very different library in the academy over the next decade. A fundamental question is whether this very different library will demand a very different librarian or information professional, and whether the philosophical roots or mainstays of librarianship will be sustained or essentially altered.

To continue this line of thinking: Academic libraries have behaved fundamentally as anticipatory libraries, selecting and acquiring information resources on a global scale in largely print/analog formats that respond to the current and anticipate the future needs of faculty and students. These materials are organized, stored, and preserved for dependable access. Library staff provide dissemination, interpretation, and instructional services to enable effective use. In the transitional or responsive academic library, these professional processes are increasingly focused on networked and interactive access to digital multimedia information at point of need, and on the innovative application of electronic technologies. Academic libraries are now implementing this model, serving as both providers of global publications and as gateways for users to resources that are increasingly created, stored, and delivered online. The library is both a historical archive and a learning and research collaborative. Clearly, how I work as a librarian has changed. But more fundamentally, has what I do and what I am also been transformed? And what are the implications for the philosophical basis of the profession?

The future academic library will carry forward these network and digital revolutions and also integrate a more market-based, customized, and entrepreneurial approach to the packaging and delivery of information. Academic libraries will become centers for research and development in the application of technology to information creation and use. They will become aggregators and publishers, and not just consumers of scholarly information. They will function as campus hubs for working with faculty on the integration of technology and electronic resources into teaching and learning. They will be providers of information services to broader academic, research, and business communities. This vision for the academic library predicts massive diversification in the models of scholarly communication and acceleration in the creation of new learning communities. This includes a redefinition of the library as a virtual resource not limited by time and space and, therefore, not as dependent on buildings for the housing, use, and servicing of information. This vision sees a repositioning of the academic library as a successful competitor in the information marketplace, and as a viable investment of financial resources by corporations, foundations, and federal agencies. Are the philosophical roots of librarianship sustained under the impact of these projected changes? Does a hybrid philosophy or perhaps an entirely new worldview come to dominate the profession? Does the profession survive?

I would argue that the fundamental question for librarianship is not survival, but really relevance and impact. Are we viewed by the users we serve as critical to their success? What roles do academic librarians play in producing successful graduates and quality scholarship? As the measure of quality moves to content plus functionality, that is, information combined with the ability to use it, and as technology assumes more and more of the functionality historically carried out by librarians, are we prepared to define new and germane activities for librarians? And as value is increasingly defined as content plus traffic, such as the number of hits on a website, and as artificial intelligence systems assume more sophisticated and expeditious guiding and reference capabilities, how does a librarian continue to play an effective role?

David Close and Carl Bridge, in their book *Revolution: A History of the Idea* (1985), argue that "the essential feel of revolution derives from its cataclysmic quality . . . it destroys people's security and unsettles their convictions." Thomas Kuhn, in *The Structure of Scientific Revolutions* (1962), observes that "the transition from a paradigm in crisis to a new one from which a new tradition can emerge is far from a cumulative process." And Karl Marx, in his theory of knowledge/ epistemology, emphasizes that ideas do not exist on their own and are real and have value only when they are translated into action, or when quantitative change produces qualitative change. This is what Marx defined as revolution. In many ways, today's academic librarian is a paradigm in crisis, unsettled, insecure, and beginning to reach that bubbling or transformational point when redefinition is both feasible and necessary.

If the virtuality of the future higher education library is to be embraced, then we must also sustain the virtuoso library, that set of professional, subject, language, technology, management, and policy skills so essential to future library vitality. We must also advance the virtuous library, built upon the wide sharing of content, technology, and expertise, the forging of expansive and innovative collaborations, and the representation of the public interest in institutional and national policy development. The virtual, virtuoso, and virtuous librarian is fundamental to our advancement of a new philosophy for the profession.

It is challenging to set the image and the understanding of librarian apart from the physical library. How does one explain the massive investments in both public and academic settings in the construction of new and the renovation of existing library spaces? We are guilty in some ways of *trompe l'oeil*, a deception of the eye, an illusion of reality in the redefinition of library as place. We may wrap the library in traditional trappings, but we are really creating new and exciting social, intellectual, and community spaces. Does this provoke the philosophy of librarianship to embrace similar qualities?

It is similarly challenging to construct a philosophy of librarianship when academic libraries are expanding the employment of individuals in professional assignments who do not have the traditional qualifying credential, the master's degree in library science. This includes hiring individuals with advanced degrees in subject disciplines, with foreign language skills, or with special technology experience, for example, into librarian positions. This includes a wide range of new professional assignments in such areas as systems, human resources, fundraising and instructional technology that demand diverse educational backgrounds. This includes the transfer of responsibilities formerly carried out by librarians to support staff and student employees. In addition, there is a new cohort of MLS librarians who have received their degrees through distance rather than residential programs. Historically, the shared graduate educational experience provided a standard preparation and a socialization into the library profession. The new professional groups have been "raised" in other environments and bring to the library a "feral" set of values, outlooks, styles, and expectations. The impact of these staffing strategies on employee relations, training, management and leadership needs to be evaluated. More fundamental is the need to understand the link to a new hybrid philosophy for the profession.

Allow me to propose a framework for thinking and talking about these various issues. We can consider eight possible responses to the opportunities for philosophical rethinking:

1. We can be naïve, not acknowledging or recognizing that we need periodic or even continuous attention to our philosophical underpinnings under the impact of fundamental if not revolutionary change.
2. We can be administrative, allowing the vagaries of the budget, the politics of the organization, or the biases of the professional leadership dictate how philosophy will be defined and communicated.
3. We can be traditional, sustaining what we have always done or how we have always thought, and not being willing to explore innovative or even provocative professional models.
4. We can be situational, changing our definitions and approaches to professional values without clear rationale or sustained commitment.
5. We can be opportunistic, gearing our philosophy to episodic conditions that support self-serving but temporary advantage.
6. We can be collaborative, shaping philosophy in the context of the complex, ambiguous, and robust relationships of cooperation and interdependence that define librarianship.
7. We can be strategic, embracing redefinition of professional philosophy as an enabling component of an agile and effective profession.
8. We can be entrepreneurial, building new roles and new markets for our assets and our expertise, and positioning librarianship for an increasingly competitive information environment.

My philosophy of librarianship demands a collaborative, strategic, and entrepreneurial approach. We must redefine the physical, expertise, and intellectual infrastructure of the profession and understand more rigorously the geography, psychology, and economics of innovation. Librarianship is legacy, traditional values, and roles that cannot be tossed away. Librarianship is infrastructure, content, expertise, spaces, and technology that enable information access and use. Librarianship is repository, conservation, and availability over time of the rich resources that define culture and progress. Librarianship is gateway, enabling global reach in a networked world to an ever-expanding and increasingly integrated body of multimedia content and tools. And librarianship is enterprise, an undertaking of phenomenal scope, complication, and risk. In this multifurcated world of librarianship, each individual member of the profession should commit to the following: a clear sense of mission, why a librarian has a distinctive and fundamental role in society; a self vision, what a librarian will achieve; a base of knowledge, what a librarian needs to understand and experience to be effective; strategic positioning, how a librarian needs to advance and participate in order to maximize impact and contribution; and continuous improvement, a commitment to personal growth and enrichment. For many who have invested their lives in librarianship, the adventure began in wonder, a sense of doubt, or perhaps curiosity or even admiration. One does not begin a life or a professional career with a sense of philosophy. These fundamental beliefs are conceptualized and formulated over time, through doing, through performance.

Reflections on a Passion

LOTSEE PATTERSON

I'M NOT EXACTLY SURE how this passion of mine for libraries came to be. It must have something to do with my childhood. I was born at the height of the Great Depression, in December 1931, on my Comanche mother's Indian allotment. A windswept, dustbowl piece of land located more than five miles over dirt roads from the nearest little town, where I attended school.

There was no library in this elementary school, not a single book that could be checked out and read. But I had books to read. My mother, a college graduate, ordered books for us to read from the state library. An early day "books by mail" program, I suppose. I can still remember the thrill of coming home and finding new books had arrived, and I recall the pleasure I had reading classics such as *Black Beauty* and *Call of the Wild*. I guess I didn't realize how exceptional that was in those days of the late 1930s and early 1940s. I grew up expecting to have books to read. The high school I attended in a different nearby town was not much better than elementary school. It had a small space with books behind a counter in the study hall where someone would hand you a book you may or may not have chosen for your English class assignment of a "book report." That was it. No browsing, no magazines, few choices.

Years later, after obtaining my bachelor's degree, I began my teaching career in a very small rural school of about one hundred students. More than 90 percent of them were American Indian and many were descendents of Geronimo's band of Apaches. It was here, I believe, that the spark that ignited my passion for libraries must have fused with my own childhood experiences. In this small school we had a few old books that no one ever read on a shelf in my classroom of seventh- and eighth-grade students. It was here that I first became aware that many students not only had no books in their homes, but they had no magazines, no newspapers, nothing to read. What could I do to change this situation? Not much. No funds were available for books; a librarian was beyond imagination. I compensated by bringing magazines from home and those contributed by my mother to the school. I particularly remember the janitor, a full-blood Apache gentleman and one of the most eloquent men I ever knew, devoured everything he could get his hands on to read. My mother saw to it he had a steady supply of reading materials. This lack of things for students to read pained me greatly as I remembered myself at this age having many memorable books to read and enjoy. If I can attribute any one thing to my lifelong fervor for libraries, it was probably this experience.

A few years later life took a turn and I found myself teaching in a Bureau of Indian Affairs (BIA) high school. This off-reservation boarding school had Indian students from more than forty-seven tribes and it had a nice library in which I worked part of each day. Working with students from reservations located all over the United States had its rewards, but I became aware of a much larger library vacuum in Indian country. As I talked with them I invariably learned their school experiences were much like I encountered in the rural school in which I had taught—no library books, no libraries. My passion was building.

This was heightened one day when a Navajo student from deep inside the Navajo reservation came toward me excitedly waving a book and exclaiming, "It's just like me, it's just like me!" He was holding a copy of Joseph Krumgold's . . . *And Now Miguel*, the story of a young boy much like himself. This student had apparently never read anything in a book with which he could directly relate his own life experience. His joy is with me to this day, and the realization that not only are books important, but books with which native students can identify became imbedded in my mind forever.

The boarding school administrators decided to send me off for one summer to take courses in library science. This turned out to be a seminal event in my life, for near the end of the summer I was offered a U.S. Department of Education Higher Education Act (HEA) Title IIB fellowship to complete my master's degree. I took leave from the boarding school, accepted the fellowship, moved my family, and became immersed in library school, never to return to the BIA school.

While in library school one of my classes had as a guest speaker, Eric Bromberg, then U.S. Department of Interior's Director of Libraries. I knew he had just published a report critical of libraries in BIA schools. We had a brief conversation about it after class. My passion was fueled again. I could not have known what effect that short exchange would have on my future.

Following graduation from library school, I decided that going back to the boarding school, with its twelve-month school year and a day that meant me leaving home at 7:00 A.M. to return at 6:00 P.M., was not a good thing for me as a single parent with five young children to raise. So, I accepted a graduate assistantship in the College of Education to work toward a doctoral degree. I rationalized that in order to send my five children to college, I was going to need a position in a college or university so my children could attend school there. It was a logical plan; it just never worked out that way. Although all of my children have college degrees, none ever attended a university where I worked.

I completed course work for the doctorate, then accepted a position with the local school district as a librarian in order to support my family. The district had moved me into the position of coordinator of libraries in my first year, and I was happily doing my work when the phone rang one day. It was the Dean of the College of Education from the University of New Mexico offering me a faculty position. I was something short of shocked because I had applied there the year before and had not received a response. I must have inquired about an interview, but he assured me they had already checked my credentials and, besides, Eric Bromberg had recommended me. The salary offered was considerably more than I was making. I accepted the offer, bought a house over the phone, moved my family, and began what was to become one of my most satisfying professional experiences.

It was in New Mexico that I finally got to act on my passion of wanting to do something to improve libraries on reservations. The year was 1972 when I began teaching at UNM, and federal monies for library-related activities were flowing. Quickly taking advantage of this, I wrote a grant that was funded to train library aides in several BIA schools in New Mexico. I knew there were no libraries in these schools, but I could not get grant money to develop one, so with a hidden agenda I proposed to train teacher's aides in basic library skills. It was my intent to cajole the school administrators into finding a space in which we could start a library in their school to make use of their newly trained "library aide." It wasn't hard to do. All of the school administrators wanted a library; they just didn't have the money for one. I simply applied my motto of "You've just got to think you can do it, and do it," which, by the way, I learned from the pilot of a small plane—I heard him mutter these words after narrowly missing a row of trees at the end of the runway! Miraculously, a small collection of materials began to find their way to our "libraries."

This work with the schools was not to last long, however, for I had no sooner begun the project than pueblo administrators sought me out. They wanted to know if I could assist them in getting a library in the pueblo. Of course I could. Another year, another grant, another hidden agenda, and I began the process of training library aides for pueblo libraries that did not exist. Libraries began to come together rather quickly; as with the schools, pueblo officials supported the idea and very much wanted a library for their people. They just needed a little help. I met with officials in each pueblo, usually starting with the pueblo councils, but was often referred to a certain individual as my liaison. Many well-intended professors, researchers, scholars and the like have failed miserably in their attempts to work with or "study Indians" because they skipped this important step of first asking Indians' permission and deferring to their guidance. I knew better and I never had a single incident of misunderstanding.

Our libraries began in a variety of locations. One shared a space with the alcohol rehab program in a century-old abandoned BIA school building, another with the food co-op, and still another with shelves placed in the tribal council meeting room. Others found space with educational programs, tribal administration, and any small room that could be cleared of previous occupants. At the end of the first year, we had libraries functioning. The process of grant writing, with some innovations to remain competitive, continued for the duration of my years at the UNM. The libraries flourished, and when I left, I had full confidence they would continue. They have and now, some thirty years later, many now have their own buildings and several of the original trainees are still managing them.

New Mexico had a number of things that contributed to its success in establishing and maintaining libraries in most of their pueblos. The grants and training I initiated were certainly the impetus for the state becoming the national model for tribal libraries, but many other factors have also contributed. First of all, the pueblo people themselves are the driving force for getting the libraries established and for slowly improving them with new materials, new facilities, and retention of library personnel. The New Mexico State Library has also been the country's leader in providing funding, training, and technical assistance for its reservation libraries. I am like a proud parent to these libraries, and while I consider them my legacy to the profession, the real force for their success is the women who have served as librarians in these pueblos. They are the ones who work with tribal councils, the state legislatures, and the state library to obtain the funding necessary to stay open; who, day to day, build programs, keep patrons returning, and band together to support one another. They are the real success story of New Mexico tribal libraries.

My departure from New Mexico was precipitated by an inability to live in such a dry climate. It caused incessant sinus problems, which could not be resolved in the arid surroundings. A move to Texas seemed a solution, and I spent seven years there. I continued to work in my own way to keep tribal libraries moving forward, but now I also concentrated on recruiting American Indians to library school. Then and now, I can claim success in that arena. Some native students I recruited are in positions as heads of medical libraries, art museum libraries, college tribal libraries, and they work in university, school, and public libraries. One is an associate professor in the library school at the University of Oklahoma. Seeing these American Indians graduate and take their place in our profession is one of my greatest pleasures. I would hasten to add that all of the minority students I recruited to library school were able to attend because they received HEA Title IIB fellowships. None of them could have obtained their degrees in library science without this federal grant program. In my opinion these fellowships have been the major factor in getting minorities into our profession.

During the 1970s and 1980s there were other important contributors to the development of libraries on reservations. Not the least of these was the National Commission on Libraries and Information Science (NCLIS). It was this body with its subcommittee on American Indians that initiated major studies of library services to Indians and which saw to it that American Indians had their own pre-conference to the White House Conference on Libraries and Information Services. I served as a consultant to the National Commission for a number of years during this period and assisted them in setting up two on-site visits to reservation libraries scattered across the nation. I accompanied the commissioners as they made their reservation visits and held regional hearings where they heard testimony from local Indian people about the need for libraries on their reservations. Some of these same people, including myself, came to Washington to testify before U.S. Congressional committees. These activities combined with the resolutions that came out of the first Indian Pre-Conference to the White House Conference led to the drafting of federal legislation that changed one title in the existing Library Services and Construction Act; it provided minimal funding for tribal libraries. I was asked to participate in drafting the legislation, and I still have the yellow legal pad on which I wrote this seminal legislation. It was adapted to federal requirements, but the original legislation was pretty much as I wrote it. This was an enormous step forward in improving tribal libraries. It remains the single most important thing that has taken place in the history of tribal library services. But there is much more to do, and I have plans for that.

Another turn in my professional life occurred when, after passage of the new legislation in 1984, officials in the U.S. Department of Education knew they needed help to successfully implement it and they issued an RFP for an outside contractor to do so. I responded through the University of Oklahoma and was awarded the contract. I left a tenured position in Texas and moved to Oklahoma, where as director of the program, I provided technical assistance and training to all tribes and Alaska villages. I called the program TRAILS (Training and Assistance for Indian Library Services). The program lasted fifteen months, during which training sessions were held throughout Indian country, a manual to assist tribes in setting up a library was written and disseminated, a core collection of titles was developed, a good discount with a vendor was negotiated, and endless phone calls requesting information and assistance were fielded. The TRAILS Manual is still in use today not only in this country but also in Canada and Australia. The TRAILS program is often mentioned when tribal libraries are the topic of conversation. Directing this program was one of the highlights of my career and was a period in which acting on my passion for developing libraries on reservations consumed my life sixteen hours a day. When a new political appointee took over the position that oversaw this program, she announced to me that she was not going to fund the TRAILS program beyond its first year because "Indians don't need libraries; they can't read anyway." The program ended and I moved on with lingering anger over this ignorant statement.

I continued to work with the National Commission as they aided American Indians in obtaining their own pre-conference to the second White House Conference on Libraries and Information Services. From 1989 to 1991, I again assisted commissioners as they conducted a second national study of tribal library services. This in-depth study resulted in an important report, "Pathways to Excellence: A Report on Improving Library and Information Services for Native American Peoples." This report contains ten recommendations for improving library services to American Indians. But soon after the report was published, the make-up of the commission changed, and they moved on to other issues leaving no strong supporter to push for legislative change to implement recommendations contained in the report.

Lacking leadership at the national level, development of tribal libraries has remained static for the past decade. There are pockets of innovation and success that are resulting in forward movement. One of these has been the advent of tribal colleges. Now numbering more than thirty, these institutions have been the genesis of renewed library development on the reservations where they reside. Tribal college libraries offer the best libraries ever to be found on their respective reservations. There is great hope here.

Some individuals, like Bonnie Biggs in California, are advancing tribal libraries. She offers assistance and encouragement to a number of tribes, and more recently she has had success in getting the state library of California to begin some activities directed toward its native communities. A group of librarians in Vancouver, British Columbia, give unselfishly of their time offering training and assistance to First Nations in developing their libraries. In the end, it is native people on the reservations who are the success story. They go about managing their small libraries and making a difference in peoples' lives every day. These are my unsung heroes and the people I admire most. I know tribal libraries will survive and grow because of their dedication.

As I reflect on my role in developing tribal libraries over the past thirty years it seems I have accomplished a lot. But I'm not quite through. I have things left to do. I am not going to quit until there is an office at the national level to provide the kind of assistance and training that the TRAILS program offered. I originally schemed that this would be a department in the U.S. Department of the Interior. But I gave up on that years ago. I toyed with the idea that I could convince the Library of Congress that they should set up such an office within their structure—a sort of American Indian Library of Congress. This office would, among other things, provide the same service to tribal government that the Congressional Research Service (CRS) provides to Congress. Why not? The tribes are sovereign nations. Don't they deserve their own CRS? But I think that idea is a bit of a stretch. My most recent and most promising choice for this re-incarnation of TRAILS is the new Smithsonian's National Museum of American Indians (NMAI). Here is a chance to get in on the ground floor and do it right. I have presented this concept to NMAI administrators and I await their actions. I'm hopeful.

These are the two things on my tribal libraries agenda for now. I'm convinced they will come to fruition and then, maybe then, I can let go of this passion of mine. But then again, I may not.

References

Biggs, Bonnie. "Strength in Numbers!" *American Libraries* 35, no. 3 (March 2004): 41–43.
Patterson, Lotsee. "Historical Overview of Tribal Libraries in the Lower Forty-Eight States." Pp. 157–162 in *Libraries to the People: Histories of Outreach*. Jefferson, N.C.: McFarland, 2003.
———. *TRAILS: Final Report*. ERIC/IR ED 278 528. Washington, D.C.: U.S. Department of Education, Office of Educational Research and Improvement, Library Programs, 1987.
———. *Tribal Library Procedures Manual*. ED 278 527. Washington, D.C.: U.S. Department of Education, Division of Library Programs, 1992.
Patterson, Lotsee, and Rhonda Taylor. "Tribally Controlled Community College Libraries: A Paradigm for Survival." *College and Research Libraries* 57 (July 1996): 316–329.
U.S. National Commission on Libraries and Information Science. *Pathways to Excellence*. Washington, D.C.: NCLIS, 1992.

Why Do Libraries Matter in the 21st Century?

MOLLY RAPHAEL

NOT LONG AGO, many pundits were predicting the end of public libraries in the United States—institutions made obsolete by technology and the Internet as well as the mega-bookstores that were opening all across our country. Even now, when I meet people in my community where libraries are thriving, I occasionally still hear this same question: "Aren't libraries going to disappear because of the Internet? I always respond with a resounding *"NO!"* I guess, in their own way, these people are asking "Why do libraries matter in the twenty-first century?"

Public libraries are enjoying a great renaissance throughout the country and especially in urban areas. My own Multnomah County Library in Portland, Oregon, has just completed a total renovation and rebuilding program. Seattle has just opened a spectacular new Central Library and is undertaking an ambitious overhaul of its branch libraries; Chicago, Los Angeles, Philadelphia, Phoenix, Jacksonville, and Nashville are a few more examples of cities where the library systems have undertaken or are in the process of completing ambitious rebuilding projects.

Why is it that so many places are rediscovering these most democratic of American institutions—open to all regardless of education, income, age, background, or views? Why do we see over and over again that communities, when given a specific choice, will vote to support their libraries? What is it about libraries that have not only won the hearts and minds of their communities, but also have frequently been able to defy the anti-tax sentiment that seems to be increasing in our country? Why would voters in economically challenged places like Tillamook County, Oregon, choose very recently to support a bond to build a new central library as well as to renew an operating levy?

The slogan "Libraries Change Lives" is not only true, but can be heard in personal stories from many people in positions of power and influence, as well as others in socially or economically challenged circumstances. I hear them every day from people I meet. The testimonials are sincere and often compelling, like the one I heard a few weeks ago when a mother of an eight-year-old told me that last summer, her son had been a poor and underachieving reader. Then her son joined our summer reading program. Thanks to the incentives and prizes that we offered, her son now reads above grade level and, this year, has brought several of his friends to the program.

Libraries have always been great equalizers in our society.

- The place where waves of immigrants and refugees, both past and present, have discovered ways of learning about American culture and adapting to their new lives.
- The place where people, during economic downturns, come to re-tool their skills or improve themselves for new opportunities.
- The place where parents with little disposable income can help their children prepare to enter school ready to learn.
- The place where small business entrepreneurs, without extensive corporate libraries and research departments, can find the information and the links they need to make smart business decisions and contribute to the economic vitality of neighborhoods.
- The place where lifelong learning thrives not only for the very young, but for the over-fifty-five population, as well as all ages in between.

These examples could go on and on. The point is that libraries have managed to hold a place in people's lives that few institutions in our society can claim. We serve our communities from womb to tomb.

Why Is This Renaissance Taking Place, and Why Now?

To begin, libraries are well-known and trusted institutions—located in communities as large and diverse as New York and Los Angeles and as small as towns of just a few thousand or even a few hundred people. We are a part of the American landscape—in fact, there are more public libraries in the United States than McDonald's. In nearly every town or community throughout our country, you can find a public library. This means that if you were born and raised in Massachusetts, you could move to Ohio when you were a teenager and find a library not too different from the one that you visited when you were growing up. Then, if you moved again to Portland, Oregon, there would be another public library in your community that, once again, offered many of the same programs and services that you had come to know in the other communities. This scenario could be repeated many times. Public libraries are ubiquitous in the United States. They are more similar than they are different. The similarities demonstrate our shared commitment to access to information; the differences reflect our need to meet the special needs of our individual communities. While libraries share common values, we know we must work closely with not only elected officials, but the many businesses, organizations, and individuals who comprise the fabric of our community.

The library's role has always been to help create an informed and thoughtful citizenry—whether through supporting children and young people who are developing early language and literacy skills, engaging in formal schooling, or expanding horizons and learning as is the out-of-school adult. What we are seeing once again, during this library renaissance, is great resilience in libraries, adapting to the changes in our society and in our individual communities indeed, thriving on the changes of the past few decades. We see these changes in our society as challenges to fulfill important community priorities, such as:

- the persistent need to learn throughout our lives;
- networked technology that makes information resources available even to the smallest of library buildings and in the homes and offices of communities;
- the significant influx of new immigrants, particularly to the metropolitan areas; and
- perhaps most overlooked by the pundits of doom, the loss of many of the places within our communities that helped bring people together in the way libraries can and do. (This opportunity is one that I call "The Library as Place".)

Let me illustrate how each of these challenges has become an opportunity for our resilient libraries.

The Need to Learn All Our Lives

Libraries are often seen as related to education and learning but not central to it. When a community leader talks about the priority of education in our communities, often the picture we have in our minds is of the K-12 school system and perhaps higher education as well. What I believe we in the library world need to do is make a more persuasive case for libraries being included in that picture, as central to lifelong learning and education.

Educators and many others already recognize the value of exposing children to the library, beginning at a very early age. Certainly, most middle-class parents make a point of taking their children to a local public library at an early age. Board books for toddlers are very popular. Most public libraries invest significant resources in children and youth services throughout the country.

But what about those kids who are in households that are not traditional library users—libraries have a mandate to serve all the people, not just the ones who happen to know about youth programs and services in our library buildings. Anyone who is in business knows that you cannot serve everyone without paying attention to what particular target constituency you are trying to serve—so we have to find the right "product" to serve the individual or organization.

Programs targeted at early childhood are expanding in public libraries. Many of us target those who have not traditionally been library users. We base our approach on brain development research, which signals the importance of emergent literacy activities at the very earliest age. We cannot wait till they are in kindergarten; we cannot even wait till they are in Headstart programs. We have to start with their parents, preparing them for parenthood. National programs such as "Born to Read," "Every Child Ready to Read," and "Raising a Reader" target very young children, their parents, and those who work with them. Reading aloud to young children appears to be the single most important activity for building understanding and skills essential for reading. Public libraries have embraced this role, frequently collaborating with educational and child development organizations.

Then, when children enter school, we continue to target underachieving readers with programs that try to make reading fun for children, with both creative programs during the school year as well as widespread public library summer reading programs. Frankly, the demand for these programs far exceeds what most libraries can support, even though school principals and teachers tell us how valuable these programs are for educational achievement.

Many of our targeted programs involve partnerships with other community organizations. Our purpose is to make a difference and that means we often will do better if we join with others. This is especially true when we reach out to immigrant and refugee communities.

Each of these activities I have just described can also be seen as contributing to workforce development. Libraries may not be leading the workforce development initiatives, but we are an important component of workforce development collaboratives.

The Amazing Opportunities of Networked Technology

The very change that threatened to bury libraries has become one of our most important assets. Bill Gates saw this when he decided, as his first effort in philanthropy, to invest in libraries, not just near Microsoft headquarters, but throughout the United States and internationally. A recent Gates Foundation report, published in collaboration with several leading nonprofit and government organizations, entitled *Toward Equality of Access: The Role of Public Libraries in Addressing the Digital Divide*, states:

> Drawing from government statistics and independent research, the report finds widespread acceptance of library-based computer and Internet access from patrons and librarians. But more importantly, the report finds that public access computing is benefiting those socioeconomic groups with the greatest need. However, the report also notes urgent—but manageable—challenges facing libraries as they seek to maintain and further develop their role in providing access to digital information. This valued public service can only be sustained by the continued support of policymakers, librarians, and community advocates.[1]

Helping to bridge the "digital divide" has become an important role for libraries all across the United States. In 1996, about 2 percent of public libraries provided access to the Internet; by 2002, that percentage had jumped to 95 percent. In fact, for those who do not have Internet access at home or in their workplace, public libraries are the most important place for access. This is even more important for low-income residents and minority groups.

For libraries, though, it was not enough for us to just offer Internet access. Librarians have also helped people access the information they were seeking. From the beginning when computers arrived in libraries, we knew that we needed to offer training and guidance in using the Internet. Basic training on the use of computers and Internet access has become part of everyday business, just as bibliographic instruction has always been a part of our role.

Some people are now saying that the Internet may not put us out of business but surely *Google* will. We all use *Google* to find information on the Internet, but libraries offer something that *Google* never will—real, live librarians to help our customers in person and online. Librarians have a passion for helping customers learn how to evaluate websites, how to narrow searches, and when and how to look for information in other, non-Internet sources.

Meeting the Needs of New Members of Our Community, Particularly New Immigrants and Refugees

This is one of the most challenging areas for libraries, but one that, no doubt, provides an opportunity to reach people who can greatly benefit from our services. Learning and understanding new cultures is not easy but is absolutely necessary if we are going to be effective. In addition, there is the obvious challenge of communicating in languages other than English. The work that national leaders such as the Queens Borough Public Library in New York (home of the melting pot) have done in this area shows us that if we invest in building bridges to these other language communities and cultures, that we will be able to meet many information, educational, and cultural needs. The work is hard because we need to build trust with these new residents. Public libraries often did not exist in the country of origin for these immigrants and refugees, and the role of government in these countries is often not one that brings a level of trust to the new home country. These new residents can benefit immensely from our resources and programs, and we must work diligently to reach them.

The Library as Place

There is no doubt that we have lost many of the places that used to bring us together in our communities. Libraries have begun to take on the role as center of community in a much more active way in recent years. This loss of place and the opportunity for civic engagement, that helps both build and bridge community, has been written about by Robert Putnam first in *Bowling Alone* and more recently in *Better Together: Restoring the American Community*. In his most recent publication, Putnam even devotes a chapter to branch libraries in Chicago, focusing on one in particular, the Near North branch, that serves the Cabrini Green public housing area as well as one of Chicago's wealthiest communities, the so-called Gold Coast on Lake Michigan. As Putnam says, "No longer a passive repository of books and information or an outpost of culture, quiet, and decorum in a noisy world, the new library is an active and responsive part of the community and agent of change."[2]

Libraries have always presented programs that try to represent different points of view, offering citizens the opportunity to engage in discussion on issues of importance and interest. With so few gathering places left in many of our neighborhoods, libraries have found that many people come to our buildings to find out what's happening and to meet and talk with others. Our meeting rooms continue to be heavily used by community organizations. In addition, we look for opportunities to present library-sponsored programs such as panel discussion on the USA Patriot Act and patriotism and dissent. Experiences in celebrating occasions like African American, Asian, and Native American Heritage Months have shown us that these events play a strong role in attracting a diverse audience who want to learn more about these cultures. This is exactly what we are trying to achieve as we help bridge from one community to another and deepen understanding of the richness of our many community cultures.

The final point I would like to make on this community building and community bridging section is that we nearly always do these programs in collaboration with other organizations. Although we often sponsor programs in our libraries, we frequently join with others in their programs rather than sponsor them ourselves.

A useful illustration of the efforts to engage the greater community is in the annual community reading projects that have sprung up all across the country, which encourage everyone in a community to read one book at the same time. In my own community, thanks to our many community partners, in January and February of each year, our reading program is everywhere. You see "Everybody Reads" on billboards, on banners, on busses, on bookstore marquees, and many, many other places. In 2004, over 16,000 teens and adults read the book *Fahrenheit 451* by Ray Bradbury, joined in book discussions, and attended over ninety events. With numerous sponsorships and community partnerships, "Everybody Reads" has wide visibility throughout the county.

Conclusion

About twenty years ago, a survey of directors of large public libraries inquired about what issues were important and consumed their time and energy. A comparison to directors of a generation earlier showed that the job bad changed dramatically, I believe a survey now would demonstrate another major change. In the mid-1980s, directors were operating in political environments and spending much of their time focused on generating support for library operations, resources, and programs.

Today, that focus on operating in a political arena is even more pronounced. We must build alliances with not only educational and cultural institutions but also business and community leaders. We must be seen as central to the health and vitality of our communities. In December 2000, an Urban Libraries Council Conference on "Partners for Successful Cities" focused on libraries as catalysts for change and economic development. At the conference, Chicago Public Library Commissioner Mary Dempsey stated very forcefully that the Chicago Public Library was not so much in the "library business" as in the "Chicago business." This statement captured, for me, the change in how we direct and lead our libraries today.

We must be catalysts for change and improvement in the communities that we serve. We must be seen not just as advocates for libraries but as "players" in the broad agenda of our cities and counties, as the late Betty Jane Narver of Seattle recognized. We can only do that if we set the strategic directions and then allow our very competent and dedicated staff to implement those strategic priorities as we engage in the broader communities that we serve. We can only be players if we engage our communities in decisions and adopt plans that support the overarching values that we share for intellectual freedom and open access, while at the same time incorporate the values and principles that are central to our own communities. Decisions that we each had to make locally in relation to Internet filtering and the Children's Internet Protection Act are excellent examples of what "playing" in the broader community means for each of us in library leadership roles.

It is indeed a very challenging and exciting time to work in public libraries!

Notes

1. *Toward Equality of Access: The Role of Public Libraries in Addressing the Digital Divide* (Seattle: Bill and Melinda Gates Foundation, 2003), 1.

2. Putnam, Robert D., and Lewis M. Feldstein, *Better Together: Restoring the American Community* (New York: Simon & Schuster, 2003), 35.

The More Things Change, the More Things Remain the Same

ANN K. SYMONS

YOU DON'T HAVE TO BE a student of library history to recognize and marvel at the changes in our profession over the last several decades and particularly in the last ten years. Since the early 1990s, technology has drastically changed the library world as we knew it, and we can assume that technological change affecting libraries will continue at the same rapid rate over the next several decades. You only have to walk into the newly opened and much celebrated Seattle Public Library to see that change has made libraries very different places than they were 100 years ago, 50 years ago, and even 10 years ago. But while the catalogs may have changed from handwritten 3 × 5 cards to Web-accessible databases, what has not changed are the profession's basic issues as identified by America's first library leaders, issues that still concern the leaders of today—serving people with books and information to match their needs, providing lifelong education, educating librarians, getting the necessary resources to build libraries where they are needed and advocating for library services.

Change Is Constant

Over the past sixty years, libraries have changed remarkably, yet as they change, the values that our profession stands for are still as firmly embedded today as they were when the Library Bill of Rights was passed by ALA's Council in 1948. I began my life as a public library user. Today, I am still a public library user. Books remain but they have been joined by just about everything else that people can read, view or listen to—videos on VHS (a format already on its way out), CDs, DVDs, MP3s, e-books, and computers that provide nearly instant access to the library's collection, to proprietary databases, and to that amazing, wacky, wonderful Internet.

When I was three I didn't know I would become a librarian. In fact I didn't know until my late twenties that I would be a librarian, and I didn't know when I was in library school learning the basic values of the librarianship that I would one day be president of the American Library Association.

As a child it wasn't possible to articulate that librarianship as a profession is based on a set of values strongly held by members of the professions who were called librarians. As an "average" librarian working out in the field it still would have been difficult articulate those values well—I just knew them when I "saw them." The profession's past and the present have been shaped by values—values that have been shared, discussed, written about, fought over, codified in ALA policies to help guide the profession, and ultimately put into practice in libraries of all type around the United States by librarians. The future, too, will be shaped by those values.

Library Values

What are the values that have informed our profession historically and into the present? I won't be here in fifty years, but I know that there will be libraries and librarians. However we continue to deliver information it will still be free, we will continue to defend the rights of people to read, view or listen to what they want, and authors and books will still exist.

We all bring different experiences in our life and our profession to our job. Every librarian's list of values may not be the same. Most library lists of values include diversity, intellectual freedom, service, privacy, literacy and lifelong learning, access, stewardship, and democracy. ALA's list of key action items for 2000–2005 includes many of those same items: intellectual freedom, democracy, privacy, diversity, twenty-first century and continuous learning, and equity of access. 2005–2006 ALA President Michael Gorman's list of values from his book *Enduring Values* are stewardship, service, intellectual freedom, rationalism, literacy and learning, equity of access, privacy and democracy. At ALA's annual conference 2004, ALA Council approved a list of core values embodied in ALA's basic policy documents: equity of access, confidentiality/privacy, democracy, diversity, education and lifelong learning, intellectual freedom, preservation, the public good, professionalism, service, social responsibility. Although all of our values are critical for us and for the communities we serve, I want to focus here on equity of access and intellectual freedom, two of our enduring and closely linked values.

Equity

In the mid 1990s, when Betty Turock became president of ALA (1995–1996), she focused her energy on an age-old theme in librarianship: equity of access. To Turock, equity in 1995 was equity on the newly emerging information superhighway. Would we as a profession be able to carve out a place for the "public good" on that highway? Would librarians rise to the challenge of providing free Internet access for patrons who did not have computers at home? The answers clearly are yes and yes as now only ten years later almost 100 percent of public libraries provide free Internet access to those they serve. Equity as a theme comes around again and again because it is clear that for libraries to provide equity of access, librarians must always keep equity issues near the top of the list of goals. Like Turock, 2003–2004 ALA President Carla Hayden also focused on equity, only this time it was equity in its broader sense. ALA published its 2004 Equity of Access brochure[1] with the following definition: "Equity of access means that all people have the information they need regardless of age, education, ethnicity, language, income, physical limitations or geographic barriers. In the late 1800s we challenged ourselves to reach out to children, immigrants, rural communities and people with visual difficulties. We are challenged today by the digital divide, the lack of access for minorities, for those who live in rural areas, and for those who do not possess basic literacy and computer skills. How do we serve the underserved in a democracy so that all have access to the information they need to live, work, and learn in their communities?

Intellectual Freedom

Equity of access depends on intellectual freedom, ". . . the right of every individual to both seek and receive information from all points of view without restriction. It provides for free access to all expressions of ideas through which any and all sides of a question, cause or movement may be explored. Intellectual freedom encompasses the freedom to hold, receive and disseminate ideas."[2]

Intellectual freedom is one of our bedrock values. The greatness of our libraries and the ALA has been our unflinching commitment to intellectual freedom. Intellectual freedom, with its high profile, is a value that has been with the profession in its present form since the late 1930s. Our commitment to this value has been tested over and over again, particularly in the last decade as we try to protect the constitutionality of the rights of young people to read and view material which is available to them on the Internet. It made me proud during my presidency to be able to honor the memory of Forrest Spaulding, author of the Library Bill of Rights. Spaulding, Director of the Des Moines [IA] Public Library wrote the Library Bill of Rights in 1938 and brought it to ALA Council for their adoption as a policy document a year later. The Library Bill of Rights as we know today was adopted from his document and approved in 1948.

My life and the lives of many of my colleagues have been shaped by something as simple as a vocal member of the community demanding that a some piece of information, book, magazine, art, exhibit be removed from the library. We all know the parent who does not want his or her child to read *Harry Potter*, Judy Blume's books, *Captain Underpants*, or *It's Perfectly Normal*. As librarians we respect that right, as well as their right to ask the library to remove items they find inappropriate. As librarians, however, we also recognize our obligation to protect the rights of all of our users to make those decisions for themselves and their families.

Along with hundreds of my colleagues, I am a *Daddy's Roommate* survivor. This book became the second most popular target of would-be censors from 1990 to 2000 according the ALA's Office for Intellectual Freedom.[3] In my case, our small community of Juneau, Alaska, was consumed for the better part of a year over whether elementary school children should be exposed to books with gay and lesbian themes.

When censorship takes on its own life in a community in the form of a major incident, it is a life-changing experience for those involved. It certainly changed mine in many ways. It made me appreciate the work of ALA's Office for Intellectual Freedom stretching back over thirty plus years. The Office for Intellectual Freedom helped me in ways that I could not provide for myself or for the librarians in my community, a service they offer to any librarian in our country. The future of librarianship, in my view, depends on a strong OIF, an OIF where members and nonmembers can take advantage of this remarkable resource for advice and help. In the Internet age many simple questions can be answered by ALA's extensive web presence in the intellectual freedom area. The complex questions are answered in the courts.

As ALA president, I focused the activities of my year around intellectual freedom. Each ALA president finds that different issues make their year both challenging and interesting, and each president's year, going back to 1876, has increased and passed on to new librarians the presence and scope of ALA, expanding the materials and programs available to all us. The most recent decade has made those resources even more accessible with the website, www.ala.org.[4] 1998–1999 was defined by tremendous controversy regarding children's access to the Internet, debate over ALA's filtering policy, and whether or not libraries should "filter." My view is that we do not help children when we simply wall them off from information and ideas that are controversial or disturbing. If they are to succeed in the Information Age, they must learn to be discerning users of information. I found during our school district's challenge that there can never be enough strong ALA documents that articulate our support for the rights of the individual.

New ALA policies in the form of intellectual freedom documents are rare. The Library Bill of Rights is rarely amended, though often explained in the form of interpretations. In 1999, the ALA Council passed a new intellectual freedom policy to add to the body of strong statements that serves our members. *Libraries: An American Value,*[5] like other ALA policies, gives librarians language they can use in promoting library services and intellectual freedom in their communities. Like other ALA documents, it was the work of a committee, this one chaired by Freedom to Read Foundation Roll of Honor recipient, June Pinnell-Stephens. Quoted in its entirety below, it is an important document because it explains the rights of library users.

Libraries: An American Value

Libraries in America are cornerstones of the communities they serve. Free access to the books, ideas, resources, and information in America's libraries is imperative for education, employment, enjoyment, and self-government.

Libraries are a legacy to each generation, offering the heritage of the past and the promise of the future. To ensure that libraries flourish and have the freedom to promote and protect the public good in the twenty-first century, we believe certain principles must be guaranteed.

To that end, we affirm this contract with the people we serve:

- We defend the constitutional rights of all individuals, including children and teenagers, to use the library's resources and services;
- We value our nation's diversity and strive to reflect that diversity by providing a full spectrum of resources and services to the communities we serve;
- We affirm the responsibility and the right of all parents and guardians to guide their own children's use of the library and its resources and services;
- We connect people and ideas by helping each person select from and effectively use the library's resources;
- We protect each individual's privacy and confidentiality in the use of library resources and services;
- We protect the rights of individuals to express their opinions about library resources and services;
- We celebrate and preserve our democratic society by making available the

widest possible range of viewpoints, opinions and ideas, so that all individuals have the opportunity to become lifelong learners—informed, literate, educated, and culturally enriched.

Change is constant, but these principles transcend change and endure in a dynamic technological, social, and political environment.

By embracing these principles, libraries in the United States can contribute to a future that values and protects freedom of speech in a world that celebrates both our similarities and our differences, respects individuals and their beliefs, and holds all persons truly equal and free.

Adopted by the Council of the American Library Association
February 3, 1999

Constitutional Challenges and Internet Concerns

In 1996, San Francisco librarians were celebrating a major First Amendment victory after the Supreme Court struck down the Communications Decency Act. Almost a decade and several lawsuits later, we are struggling with unresolved questions resulting from that decision.

We have been able to use our continuing challenges of the constitutional rights involved with Internet access to remind our library users, members of the public, legislators, and others of the principles that libraries and librarians represent.

The questions and concerns raised by the Internet challenge us to examine and reconcile some of our core principles and practices as a profession. They also provide a huge opportunity to educate library users, legislators, and other members of the public about this new technology, the role of libraries, and the First Amendment.

How can our society protect children from materials that clearly are not appropriate for them? What materials should tax dollars pay for anyway? How much access is too much? What is the role of librarians? There are no easy answers.

These questions are not unanticipated, nor are they new. They do give us what we in the classroom call "a teachable moment." The questions being raised relate directly to one of our responsibilities: to educate as well as provide access to information.

The Internet is neither good nor evil. It is simply a tool, one that we as a society are learning to understand and to use. As librarians, we must be leaders in educating both children and adults about the benefits and hazards of this new medium and how to use it wisely.

Much has been made of ALA's filtering resolution, the protection of children versus the values of intellectual freedom and the First Amendment, and the requirement of filters in libraries to receive federal funding. The best and ultimate filter is the human mind. Knowing how to make informed decisions about what we choose to see, hear, and view is an essential skill in the Information Age— whether it's in the library, at school, at work, or at home.

ALA's leadership has put a big spotlight on how librarians are helping to guide parents and children in cyberspace. ALA is the voice for millions of children, teenagers, and adults who depend on them for free access to information.

The debate over Internet access has continued for many years. It will continue as long as we see new technology and change, continue in our communities, over the airwaves, and among us as professionals. If we cannot resolve the questions in such a way that protects all of our rights and recognizes our differing information needs, we will resolve them in our courts.

Protecting the First Amendment in the digital environment is worthy of our time, best professional efforts, and financial resources.

Forrest Spaulding—Yesterday, Today, and Tomorrow

I deliberately titled this essay "The More Things Change, the More They Stay the Same." The library where Forrest Spaulding worked in Iowa in 1938 is not the library that any of us work in today. But Spaulding's dedication to the principles of intellectual freedom embodied in his first documents remains as strong a guiding value today as it was in 1938. Thank you, Forrest Spaulding for what you have done for generations of librarians and library users. We may not often remember your name but your principles are put into practice daily. By 2050 we may be dealing with different intellectual freedom issues but I am confident that the underlying principles will be the same.

As a child I had no idea who Forrest Spaulding was and no idea I would become a librarian as an adult. My child's view of the library was that I liked it, the books were good to read, and I could go every week. The Stockton (CA) Public Library, full of wonderful things to read, had librarians to help me find what I wanted, and the best part was that everything was free. Our family had only to get a library card for the world to open up to us. We couldn't afford to buy books, and I don't even remember a bookstore as a constant in my youth. I didn't know that some libraries had rules that "children" couldn't go into the adult section. My parents encouraged me to read widely, and the librarians never stopped me from checking out anything that I wanted. My experience as a child represents many of our enduring values, including service, equity of access, and intellectual freedom. These values continue to mould the profession and will provide the heart of libraries in the decades to come.

Notes

1. American Library Association, *Equity of Access*, ALAAction No. 5 (2004), www.ala.org/ala/ourassociation/governingdocs/keyactionareas/equityaction/equitybrochure.htm.

2. American Library Association, Office for Intellectual Freedom, *Intellectual Freedom and Censorship Q & A*, www.ala.org/ala/oif/basics/intellectual.htm (2004).

3. American Library Association, Office for Intellectual Freedom, *The 100 Most Frequently Challenged Books of 1990–1999*, www.ala.org/ala/oif/bannedbooksweek/bbwlinks/top100challenged.htm (2004).

4. American Library Association, www.ala.org, (2004).

5. American Library Association, *Libraries: An American Value*, http://www.ala.org/ala/oif/statementspols/americanvalue/librariesamerican.htm (1999).

References

Gorman, Michael. *Our Enduring Values: Librarianship in the 21st Century*. Chicago: American Library Association, 2000.

Speaking Out: Voices in Celebration of Intellectual Freedom. Chicago: American Library Association, 1999.

About the Contributors

The Editor

Norman Horrocks is professor emeritus, School of Library and Information Studies (SLIS), Dalhousie University, Halifax, Nova Scotia; editorial consultant and series editor for Scarecrow Press; and a contributing editor for *Library Journal*. He has a B.A. in constitutional history (Western Australia), an MLS, and a Ph.D. (Pittsburgh); is a Fellow of the Chartered Institute of Library and Information Professionals (U.K.) and an Associate of the Library Association of Australia.

Norman has worked in libraries in Manchester (England), Cyprus, and Western Australia and has taught in Australia, at Perth; in the United States, at Pittsburgh, Hawaii, and Rutgers—the State University of New Jersey; and in Canada, at Dalhousie University, where he was Director of SLIS and Dean of the Faculty of Management before becoming Vice President—Editorial at Scarecrow Press (1986–1995). He was an external examiner for the Library School at the University of the West Indies and has spoken there and at many other international gatherings.

Norman has been elected or appointed to office in numerous LIS and related organizations in the United Kingdom, Australia, the United States, and Canada, and has been a contributor to or editor of a number of their journals. He has been elected to honorary membership of the American, British, and Canadian library associations as well as the Atlantic Provinces and the Nova Scotia associations. The Nova Scotia Library Association has established a Norman Horrocks Library Leadership Award. Other awards have included those from the American Library Association, the Association for Library and Information Science Education, Beta Phi Mu, New Jersey Library Association, Rutgers University, the University of Pittsburgh, and the Kaula Gold Medal and Citation (India).

The Contributors

Ismail Abdullahi is an associate professor at Clark Atlanta University, School of Library and Information Studies, Atlanta, Georgia. He is a graduate of the Royal

School of Library and Information Science, Denmark; has an MLS from North Carolina Central University; and a Ph.D. from the University of Pittsburgh. Prior to his CAU appointment, he was on the faculty at the University of Southern Mississippi. He has worked as a librarian in public, special, and academic libraries in Denmark and the United States and as a library consultant in Denmark, the United States, and the United Kingdom.

Adviser to the Diversity Group of the Chartered Institute of Library and Information Professionals in the United Kingdom, Dr. Abdullahi has conducted many seminars and workshops on diversity issues in various cities in Europe. He has received the Harold Lancour Award for Excellence in International and Comparative Study in Library and Information Science, the Meyers Center Award for the Study of Human Rights in the United States, a Leadership Award from the Black Caucus of the American Library Association, and numerous awards from community associations. He is active in the American Library Association, where he is an elected member of its Council, the Association for Library and Information Science Education, the Black Caucus of the American Library Association, the Special Libraries Association, the International Federation of Library Associations and Institutions, and the Metro Atlanta Library Association.

Camila Alire is dean of university libraries at the University of New Mexico, Albuquerque. Previously, she was dean emeritus at Colorado State University in Fort Collins and was dean/director of libraries at the Auraria Library, University of Colorado at Denver for six years. She received her doctorate in higher education administration from the University of Northern Colorado, holds an MLS from the University of Denver, and a B.A. from Adams State College, Alamosa, Colorado. She is president-elect of ACRL and will assume office as president in June 2005. She is chair of the executive committee for the ACRL 2005 National Conference in Minneapolis. She has chaired several ALA committees, served on four ALA President's Special Advisory Task Forces and on ALA Council and Executive Board. She was president of REFORMA (National Association to Promote Library and Information Services to Latinos and the Spanish Speaking) in 1994–1995 and was named REFORMA Librarian of the Year in 1997.

Camila's research focuses on library services for Latinos and other minorities, on library disaster recovery, and on recruitment and retention of minorities in the library profession and in higher education. She has given workshops and talks on leadership development, library advocacy, and on library services to Latino communities. She co-authored (with Orlando Archibeque) *Serving Latino Communities* and contributed to and edited *Library Disaster Planning and Recovery Handbook*. She was chosen to be included in the ALA/ALTA National Advocacy Honor Roll

2000. In 1999, she was named Scholar-in-Residence for the Chicago Public Library System. She was awarded the first ALA Elizabeth Futas Catalyst for Change Award and National REFORMA's Librarian of the Year in 1997. In 1998, she was named one of the 100 most influential Hispanics in the country by *Hispanic Business Magazine*.

John N. Berry III is editor-in-chief of *Library Journal*, where he has been employed since 1964. A graduate of Boston University, he earned his MS in library science at Simmons College in Boston. Berry has served as reference librarian and young adult librarian in Reading (MA) Public Library and reference librarian and administrator at the Simmons College Library. He has taught in the LIS programs at Louisiana State University, the University of Washington, Simmons College, and the University of Pittsburgh and teaches currently in LIS programs at Dominican University, Pratt Institute, and the University of Arizona. He is the winner of the American Library Association's Joseph W. Lippincott Award, the Association for Library and Information Science Education Service Award, and, as editor of the *Bay State Librarian*, the ALA/H. W. Wilson Company Library Periodical Award. The Simmons College School of Library Science gave him the First Annual Alumni Achievement Award in 1970.

Toni Carbo is a professor at the School of Information Sciences (SIS) and Graduate School of Public and International Affairs, University of Pittsburgh, where she teaches Understanding Information (the introductory course for LIS), Information Ethics, and Information Policy. From 1986 to 2002, she was the dean of SIS. From 1980 to 1986, she was executive director of the U.S. National Commission on Libraries and Information Science, following work with abstracting and information services in the United States and the United Kingdom, and in libraries at Brown University, the University of Washington, and the American Mathematical Society. She has an A.B. from Brown University and an MS and Ph.D. from Drexel University. Toni is a Fellow of the American Association for the Advancement of Science, the Institute of Information Scientists, the National Federation of Abstracting and Information Services, and the Special Libraries Association. She is a member of the boards of the Center for Democracy and Technology, and Three Rivers Connect, and a past-president of the American Society for Information Science & Technology and the Association for Library and Information Science Education. Toni edits *The International Information and Library Review* and is the author of numerous publications.

Toni has been honored by receiving major awards from the American Society for Information Science & Technology, the Association for Library and Information Science Education, and the Centennial Medal from Drexel University as one of its 100 most distinguished alumni; was appointed as the first Madison Council Fellow in Library and Information Science at the Library of Congress in 2002; and has been recognized by Governor Edward G. Rendell as a Distinguished Daughter of Pennsylvania in 2004.

Mary K. Chelton is a professor in the Graduate School of Library and Information Studies, Queens College, City University of New York. She received her doctorate from the Graduate School of Communication, Information and Library Studies at Rutgers—the State University of New Jersey with a dissertation on adult-adolescent service encounters. An award-winning librarian prior to her doctorate, Chelton's primary research focus is on marginalized users and services in library contexts. In this regard, she is particularly interested in the information-seeking of adolescents, adoption searchers, readers advisory services for adults, and popular culture genres. Besides starting *Voice of Youth Advocates* magazine with Dorothy Broderick, she has published over fifty journal articles on various aspects of library services, including, "Readers' Advisory 101: Common Mistakes in Readers Advisory Work and How to Avoid Them" (*Library Journal*, November 1, 2003), "Five-Foot Bookshelf: Most Important Professional Books for Young Adult Librarians of the Last Year," (*VOYA*, October 2003), "What Kind of Romance Are You in the Mood For? A Recommended Reading List," with Cathie Linz, Joyce Saricks, Lynne Welch, and Ann Bouricious (*Booklist*, September 15, 2001), and "Reader's Advisory: Matching Mood and Material," (*Library Journal*, February 1, 2001) with Catherine Sheldrick Ross. Besides introducing and editing three successive compilations of YA programs for ALA, the Excellence in Library Services for Young Adults books, she also edited three volume years of the first readers advisory column in *RUSA Quarterly* and a book on youth information-seeking behavior with Colleen Cool. A frequent speaker and conference organizer on YA and RA services topics, Mary K. is currently owned by two Vizslas and lives on Long Island with her partner and *VOYA* cofounder, Dorothy M. Broderick.

Ginnie Cooper joined Brooklyn Public Library as executive director in January 2003. She oversees a network of sixty libraries, including the Grand Army Plaza Library and neighborhood libraries throughout the borough, as well as the creation of BPL's new Visual and Performing Arts Library. Ginnie works with elected officials and the Brooklyn Public Library Foundation to provide the best in library services to the 2.5 million residents of Brooklyn.

Ginnie was director of the Multnomah County Library in Portland, Oregon, for thirteen years. From 1981 to 1990, she served as director of Alameda County Library in Fremont, California, and has also worked in libraries and schools in Minnesota, Wisconsin, and South Dakota. A librarian since 1970, Ginnie earned an MLS from University of Minnesota. She is a past president of the Public Library Association, a division of the American Library Association. She is a recipient of the Charlie Robinson Award made by the Public Library Association to recognize a public library director who has been a risk-taker, an innovator, and an agent for change.

Leigh S. Estabrook is professor of library and information science and of sociology at the University of Illinois, Urbana–Champaign. From 1986 to 2001, she served as dean of the Graduate School of Library and Information Science at UIUC. Estabrook received her Ph.D. in sociology from Boston University, MS in library science from Simmons College, and A.B. in history from Northwestern University. Leigh directs the Library Research Center with which she currently conducts research about the impact of the USA Patriot Act on libraries and changes in scholarly communication in the humanities. She is a frequent contributor to library literature and active consultant to libraries and library vendors. Among her recent honors are the 2003 Association for Library and Information Science Award (ALISE) for professional contributions to library and information science education and the 2002 Beta Phi Mu Award from the American Library Association and Beta Phi Mu. She is also a past president of ALISE and a Fellow of the A. K. Rice Institute.

Barbara J. Ford is director of the Mortenson Center for International Library Programs and Mortenson Distinguished Professor at the Library of the University of Illinois at Urbana–Champaign. She was the 1997–1998 president of the American Library Association and her theme was "Libraries: Global Reach, Local Touch." Barbara previously worked as assistant commissioner for central library services at the Chicago Public Library, director of the Virginia Commonwealth University libraries, and associate library director at Trinity University in San Antonio, Texas. She served in several capacities at the University of Illinois at Chicago and was director of the Soybean Insect Research Information Center at the Illinois Natural History Survey. She was a Peace Corps Volunteer in Panama and Nicaragua. She was president of the Association of College and Research Libraries, a division of the ALA, from 1990 until 1991. She currently is a member of the International Federation of Library Associations and Institutions (IFLA) Section on University Libraries and Other General Research Libraries. She previously served as the secretary for the IFLA Section on Government Information and Official Publications. As the author of publications and presentations, Barbara has traveled around the world to address topics such as information literacy, government information, the future of libraries, the role of library associations, and international cooperation among libraries.

Barbara earned a B.A. in history and education from Illinois Wesleyan University, a Master's degree in international relations from the Fletcher School of Law and Diplomacy at Tufts University, and a master's degree in library science from the University of Illinois at Urbana–Champaign.

Michael Gorman is dean of library services at the Henry Madden Library, California State University, Fresno. From 1977 to 1988, he worked at the Library of the University of Illinois, Urbana as director of technical services, director of general services, and acting university librarian, successively. From 1966 to 1977, he was head of cataloguing at the British National Bibliography, a member of the British Library Planning Secretariat, and head of the Office of Bibliographic Standards in the British Library, successively. He has taught at library schools in Britain and in the United States. He is the first editor of the Anglo-American cataloguing rules, second edition (1978), and of the revision of that work (1988). He is the author of *The Concise AACR2, 3rd Edition*; *Future Libraries: Dreams, Madness, and Reality* (1999, cowritten with Walt Crawford); and *Our Enduring Values*, published by ALA in 2000, which was the winner of the 2001 Highsmith Award for the best book on librarianship. Michael is the author of hundreds of articles in professional and scholarly journals. He has contributed chapters to a number of books and is the author or editor of other books and monographs. He has given numerous presentations at international, national, and state conferences.

Michael has been the recipient of numerous awards, including the Margaret Mann Citation in 1979, the 1992 Melvil Dewey Medal, and Blackwell's Scholarship Award in 1997. He was made a Fellow of the [British] Library Association in 1979 after his studies at Ealing Technical College, now Thames Valley University, and elected as an Honorary Fellow of Britain's Chartered Institute of Library and Information Professionals in 2004. Twice elected to the Council of the American Library Association, Michael will serve as its president for 2005–2006.

Ken Haycock is a professor at the University of British Columbia and senior partner with Ken Haycock & Associates, Inc. He was formerly a member of the senior management team with the Vancouver (British Columbia) School Board. Ken has a B.A. in political science and a Dip.Ed. from the University of Western Ontario, and holds master's degrees in education (Ottawa), library and information studies (Michigan), and business administration (Royal Roads); his doctorate is from Brigham Young University. Ken began his career as a secondary school history teacher and teacher librarian at Glebe Collegiate Institute in Ottawa and was a department head at Colonel By Secondary School in Ottawa. Later he moved to Guelph as educational media specialist for the Wellington County Board of Education. In 1976, he moved to British Columbia as coordinator for the Vancouver School Board's more than one hundred school libraries, district resource services, and special libraries. Later he became a member of Vancouver's senior management team responsible for curriculum and program development and implementation for 7,000 employees at 115 sites while also principal of a large elementary school. In 1992, he returned to librarianship as a tenured professor and director of the School of Library, Archival and Information Studies at the University of British Columbia for two five-year terms.

Ken is a past president of the American Association of School Librarians, the Canadian Library Association, and the Canadian School Library Association, and is the 2005–2006 president of the Association for Library and Information Science Education. He has also been an elected member of the Council and Executive Board of the American Library Association and chair of the Section on Education and Training of the International Federation of Library Associations and Institutions. An active community member, Ken has also been a public library trustee on two occasions, an elected school board chair and municipal councilor. A prolific writer and researcher, Ken has been honored with awards from the American Library Association (White Award for Promoting Librarianship) and the Canadian Library Association (Outstanding Service Award and Honorary Life Membership), among others. Phi Delta Kappa named him an outstanding young educator and the Governor-General of Canada conferred the Queen Elizabeth II Silver Jubilee Medal for contributions to Canadian society.

Patrick Jones runs Connectingya.com, a firm dedicated to consulting, training, and coaching for providing powerful youth services. He is the author (with Michele Gorman and Tricia Suellentrop) of *Connecting Young Adults and Libraries, 3rd Edition* (2004), which is considered "the bible" of young adult services. He has also published *A Core Collection for Young Adults* (2003), *Running A Library Card Campaign: A How to Do It Manual* (2002), and *Do It Right: Customer Service for Young Adults in School and Public Libraries* (2001). He has been involved for years in the Young Adult Library Services Association, a division of the American Library Association, and was the writer for YALSA's book *New Directions in Library Service to Young Adults* (2002). This document provides the broad philosophical framework for serving young adults in school and public libraries. He has also authored the first volume in Scarecrow's Studies in Young Adult Literature series *What's So Scary* *about R. L. Stine?* He is a frequent speaker at library conferences and has trained library staff in all fifty states, as well as in Canada, Australia, and New Zealand. In spring 2004, he published his first young adult novel entitled *Things Change.*

Gillian McCombs is currently the dean and director of Central University Libraries, at Southern Methodist University in Dallas, Texas. With a B.A. (Honours) in French and European Literature from the University of Warwick and a master's degree from the Leeds School of Librarianship, Gillian began her professional career in England as the music librarian in Huddersfield Public Library, in her native Yorkshire. Her career in the United States has taken her from Washington D.C.—where she worked at the Landscape Architecture and Garden Library at Dumbarton Oaks, as well as numerous federal libraries such as the National Library of Medicine, the Federal Reserve, and the Department of the Interior—to the University at Albany, State University of New York (SUNY), where she was assistant director for technical services and systems. She received her MPA from the University at Albany in 1995. Gillian has won numerous professional honors, including the Chancellor's Award for Excellence in Librarianship, SUNY (1997), the University at Albany President's Award for Librarianship (1997), the Eastern New York/ACRL Librarian of the Year Award (1998), and the Distinguished Service Award from the Hudson Mohawk Library Association in 1997. She was selected to participate in the prestigious Association of Research Libraries (ARL) Senior Fellows program in 1995 and for Leadership America in 2003. She has a substantial record of speaking and scholarly publication, having written and presented on the topics of fundraising, information technology, academic librarianship, historical children's literature, organizational culture, leadership, and management. She is currently past chair of the University Libraries Section of ACRL, chair of the board of advisors for the School of Library and Information Sciences at the University of North Texas, and president of SMU's Town and Gown Club.

Kathleen de la Peña McCook is Distinguished University Professor at the University of South Florida where she has also been director at the School of Library and Information Science. She has held administrative and faculty positions at Louisiana State University and the University of Illinois, Urbana. She holds a Ph.D. from the University of Wisconsin–Madison; master's degrees from Marquette University (English) and the University of Chicago (library science), and a B.A. in English from the University of Illinois–Chicago. She has been president of the Association for Library and Information Science Education and was the 2002 Latino Librarian of the Year (Trejo Award). She has received the Beta Phi

Mu Award for distinguished service to education for librarianship; the ALA Elizabeth Futas Catalyst for Change Award; the ALA RUSA-Margaret E. Monroe Adult Services Award; the ALA Equality Award; and the ALA Library Diversity Research Award. In 2003, Kathleen was Scholar-in-Residence at the Chicago Public Library. Her recent publications include *Introduction to Public Librarianship* (2004), *A Place at the Table: Participating in Community Building* (2000), *Ethnic Diversity in Library and Information Science* (2000), *Library Services to Youth of Hispanic Heritage* (2000), and *Women of Color in Librarianship* (1998).

James G. (Jim) Neal is currently the vice president for information services and university librarian at Columbia University, New York, providing leadership for university academic computing and network services and a system of twenty-five libraries. He also works with the Electronic Publishing Initiative at Columbia (EPIC) and the Columbia Center for New Media Teaching and Learning (CCN-MTL). He serves on key academic, technology, budget, and policy groups at Columbia. Previously, he served as the dean of university libraries at Indiana University and at Johns Hopkins University, and held administrative positions in the libraries at Penn State, Notre Dame, and the City University of New York. At Columbia, he has focused in particular on the development of the digital library, special collections, global resources, instructional technology, building construction/renovation, and fundraising programs. Jim has served on the Council and Executive Board of the American Library Association, on the board and as president of the Association of Research Libraries (ARL), and as chair of OCLC's Research Library Advisory Council. He currently is chair of the board of directors of the Research Libraries Group (RLG) and on the board of the National Information Standards Organization (NISO). He has also served on numerous international, national, and state professional committees and is an active member of the International Federation of Library Associations and Institutions (IFLA).

Jim is a frequent speaker at national and international conferences, consultant, and published researcher with a focus in the areas of scholarly communication, intellectual property, digital library programs, organizational change, staff turnover, and fundraising. He has served on the editorial boards of journals in the field of academic librarianship and on the Board of Project Muse, the electronic journal publishing program at Johns Hopkins, on the advisory board for the E-History Book Project at the American Council of Learned Societies, on the advisory board of PubMed Central at the National Institutes of Health, on the Scholarly Communication Committees of ARL and ACRL, as chair of the steering committee of SPARC, the Scholarly Publishing and Academic Resources Coalition, and currently serves on the board of the Columbia University Press. He has represented the American library community in testimony on copyright matters before Congressional committees and was an advisor to the U.S. delegation at the World Intellectual Property Organization (WIPO) diplomatic conference on copyright. He has worked on copyright policy and advisory groups for universities and professional and higher education associations. He was selected the 1997 Academic/Research Librarian of the Year by ALA's Association of College and Research Libraries.

Lotsee Patterson is professor of library and information studies at the University of Oklahoma. Previously she was on the faculty at the University of New Mexico and Texas Woman's University. An enrolled member of the Comanche Nation, she currently serves as chair of the Comanche Nation College Board. A consultant to Indian tribes across the nation, she works tirelessly to develop and improve libraries in Indian Country. Her advocacy crosses international borders where she collaborates on library issues with indigenous people around the world. She has also served as a special advisor to the Smithsonian's National Museum of the American Indian (NMAI) and to the National Commission on Libraries and Information Science (NCLIS). She was a founder of the American Indian Library Association, of which she has been president, vice president, and editor of the association's newsletter.

Lotsee's American Library Association activities have included committee membership with many ALA divisions including the Office of Literacy and Outreach Services (OLOS), the Committee on Accreditation (COA), and currently Spectrum's National Advisory Committee. She has delivered one of the Jean Coleman lectures at the annual ALA conference.

In 2005, Lotsee was elected to Honorary Membership, the highest award of the American Library Association. Earlier awards include the Oklahoma Library Association's Distinguished Service Award; NCLIS's Silver Award; the American Library Association's Equality and Beta Phi Mu awards, and the New Mexico Library Association, Native American Libraries Special Interest Group's Founders Award.

Molly Raphael was appointed director of libraries for Multnomah County in the fall of 2003. Molly joins Multnomah County Library from the District of Columbia Public Library, where she served as director for almost six years. She began her library career at the District of Columbia Public Library as an assistant children's librarian in 1970 and held several leadership positions within that system prior to becoming its director. A recognized leader in the library field, Molly has been an active member of the American Library Association since 1974.

Recently she completed a term on its governing board and is continuing on its legislative body. Molly's professional activities have also included serving as president of the District of Columbia Library Association and as cofounder of the ALA's Forum for Library Service to People with Hearing Impairments. She is a member of the Urban Libraries Council, the Freedom to Read Foundation, and the Friends of Libraries USA.

Molly holds a B.A. from Oberlin College and a master's degree in library science from Simmons College.

Ann K. Symons is a conference speaker, author, and library consultant. She was employed by the Juneau [AK] School District from 1972 to 1998 as a librarian at both the elementary and secondary level. Before living in Alaska, she was a catalog librarian at Oregon State University. Ann holds a B.A. from the University of California Davis (1965), an MLS from the University of Oregon (1970), and a Certificate in Advanced Studies in Librarianship from the University of Denver. She has been both president and treasurer of the American Library Association, a member of the ALA Executive Board, a member of ALA Council, and chair of ALA's Intellectual Freedom Committee. Ann's association activities also included board and officer positions in the Alaska Library Association, the Alaska Association of School Librarians, and Authors to Alaska. Symons' major honors include: ALA Joseph W. Lippincott Award (2002), Robert B. Downs Intellectual Freedom Award (2000), ALA Elizabeth Futas Catalyst for Change Award (2000), AASL/SIRS Intellectual Freedom Award (1996), and Freedom to Read Foundation Roll of Honor Award (1994).

The coauthor of *Protecting the Right to Read: A How-to-Do-It Manual for School and Public Librarians* (1995, with Charles Harmon) and the coeditor of *Speaking Out: Voices in Celebration of Intellectual Freedom* (1999, with Sally Gardner Reed), Ann has also published numerous articles in library publications. Over the last ten years, she has spoken to library associations, leadership institutes, and external groups in forty states and several countries.